Dead Man's Clothes

DEDICATION

For my mother, Fannie Jeanette Boersma Davidson

I have always known that mom likes me the best, but if you ask any one of my siblings, four brothers and three sisters, they would disagree and insist that mom likes them best. She always had time for us and made each of us feel special.

Dead man's Clothes

The Bum Camp of
Tolt, Washington

Dale L. Davidson

hancock
house

ISBN 0-88839-608-2
EAN 9780888396082
Copyright © 2006 Dale L.Davidson

Cataloging in Publication Data

Davidson, Dale, 1939–
    Dead man's clothes : the bum camp of Tolt, Washington /
    Dale Davidson.

    ISBN 0-88839-608-2

    1. Davidson, Dale, 1939–. 2. Carnation (Wash.) — Biography.
3. Tramps — Washington (State) — Carnation — History. I. Title.

F899.T64D38 2005   979.7'77   C2005-905564-2

Printed in Indonesia — TK PRINTING

Editing: Nancy Miller
Production: Mia Hancock
Illustrations: Allen Miller
Cover design: Rick Groenheyde
Front cover illustration: Allen Miller ("Dutch Stew," page 26)
Back cover Illustration: Allen Miller ("Whizzer Motorbike," page 41)

Published simultaneously in Canada and the United States by

HANCOCK HOUSE PUBLISHERS LTD.
19313 Zero Avenue, Surrey, B.C. Canada V3S 9R9
(604) 538-1114 Fax (604) 538-2262

HANCOCK HOUSE PUBLISHERS
1431 Harrison Avenue, Blaine, WA U.S.A 98230-5005
(604) 538-1114 Fax (604) 538-2262

Website: **www.hancockhouse.com**
Email: **sales@hancockhouse.com**

Contents

PART I — Bum Camp

PART II — Stories from the Farm

Preface

Relating my childhood stories over the last several years, more and more people would tell me I should write a book. Now, I know I am a better storyteller than I am a writer, but I'll do my best to take you up the railroad tracks and into the world of my early days. Come with me into the camp and meet some of the people that were my friends, those bums that were wearing some dead man's clothes.

They came by bus
Those bums in rags
To the camp across the tracks.

They were bathed and fed
And dressed in a suit
A gift from a dead man …his clothes.

They were given a cot and a blanket
Plus three meals a day
At the camp across the tracks.

Nobody knows where they came from
They kept to their selves
These bums that were wearing
A gift from a dead man...his clothes.

They could come and go
At the place they call home
The camp across the tracks.

They closed the place
The bums called home
The camp across the tracks.

They left by bus
To live on the streets
Those bums that were wearing
Some dead man's clothes.

Acknowledgments

I want to thank Lorrie Harrison and her son, Robert, for liking my book and encouraging me early on, as well as my daughter-in-law, Lynn, who encouraged me to "just write." She's a good teacher and I think that is the best advice that a teacher could give. Also, I want to thank my daughters. April, without her typing I wouldn't have a damn book, Diana, for her encouragement and finding photos and Jamie for her continuous loving support. For all of the illustrations in this book, which bring these stories to life, I thank my lifelong friend Allen Miller. A big thanks to the Milwaukee Railroad for all my brothers and sisters, because it was that late train that would wake Mom and Dad, and many times they couldn't go back to sleep. Shorty played an important role in me writing this book because when I started thinking of him, I started writing. And, last but not least, I want to thank my wife, Debra, for her support.

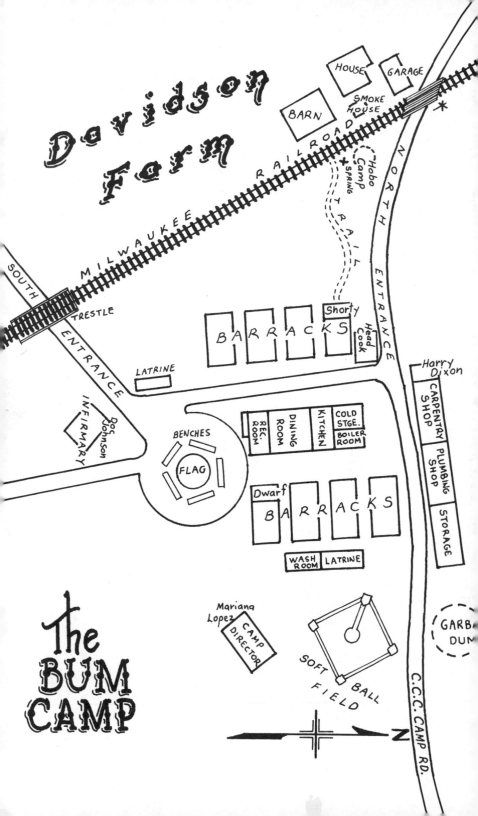

Part I
Bur Camp

Tolt, Washington

January 11, 1939, my parents drove to Seattle's Harborview Hospital so that I could be born. I arrived on January 12. The drive from Tolt, about thirty-five miles east of Seattle, was no easy task. There were no bridges yet on Lake Washington, so you would catch a ferry at Kirkland or drive around the north end of the lake to Bothell/Kenmore or south through Renton. My folks took me home to the Snoqualmie Valley where my sister Donna, four, and my brother Larry, two, were waiting for us.

Mom and Dad bought the homestead in 1935 from Weyerhaeuser—thirteen acres for $500. They paid fifty dollars a year for ten years with no interest. My dad ran a trapline for muskrat and mink, mostly, to pay for the property. They hand-cleared it with the help of my granddad's draft horses, Rock and Rye, named after the drink rye on the rocks. (Grandpa Boersma must have bought the team already named because he didn't drink at all.) The trees on the property provided the lumber for the house that they built in 1937. My mom and brother Joe still live in that house today.

The home place is located two miles south of Tolt (Carnation) on the Fall City-Carnation Highway. When I was school age, Tolt had a population of approximately 200. And by the time I was in high school, it had grown to about 450. Sometime in the 1950s there was a push from Carnation Farms to change the town name from Tolt to Carnation. The employees of Carnation Farms were given the day off to vote, but the Tolt townsfolk didn't think it would ever happen and didn't bother to vote. The vote passed, and since then the town has been known as Carnation, although the old timers still call it Tolt. The high school was called Tolt, and the middle school is still Tolt to this day.

The Snoqualmie Valley was the perfect place to grow up. The Snoqualmie River runs the length of the valley and joins the Skykomish River in Monroe, thus becoming the Snohomish River that runs into Puget Sound at Everett. This lush valley was home to more than thirty dairy farms, orchards and berry farms back then, most are gone now.

We had a co-op before anyone ever knew what a co-op was. The Reichmann's, a local family, owned a cannery and canned for "Picksweet Foods." They canned peas, corn, green beans, etc., and at the end of the season they let several families bring their fruit and produce to be canned and traded. Our family would trade beans and squash for corn and everyone had apples for sauce. The only cost to us was the half-cent to three-cents per can, depending on the size of the can. We didn't pay anything for the actual canning of the produce. We also canned salmon and steelhead. The woods were full of game, so we would harvest a few deer every year.

The Grange Store in Tolt was owned and operated by

the Grange members of lower Snoqualmie Valley. The front of the store was groceries and clothing and the middle of the store had hardware. Nails wire, tools and wheelbarrows were next. In the far back of the big, long building was the feed mill. At the back was a railroad spur that the grain and molasses railcars parked along. They would mix all the feeds and sack it up, and we would go there for all our feed.

I remember one time the town's Italian families had a rail car of grapes sent up from California. The juice from the crates of big red wine grapes was dripping out of the car on the ground, but soon the grapes were crushed and fermenting on the way to becoming "Dago red," the beverage of choice for most Italian families in our area.

The Milwaukee Railroad tracks were within forty feet of the back of our house and within twenty feet of the garage and barn. The right-of-way ran the full length of our property. Across the tracks was an old logging camp that had been updated and used by the CCC (Civilian Conservation Corps, part of Franklin Roosevelt's New Deal programs that provided work and vocational training for unemployed, single young men). Around 1934, the camp became the State of Washington Convalescent Home, known to the locals as "the bum camp."

When my folks brought me home from the hospital, Mom tells that there were four bums at the livingroom window wanting to see the new baby. The group was led by Dutch, hat in hand, explaining that they had seen lots of newborns but not a human newborn. Thus, I first met Dutch, and he became my friend through all my early years.

As soon as I was old enough to leave our yard, I would check on my three favorite things: the railroad trestle, the bum camp and Griffin Creek. My brother Larry, two years

Harborview where I was born in 1939.

The wagon we used in our wine bottle resale business, when it was new.

older than me, and my cousin Gary, two years younger, were my sidekicks. Early in the morning the freight train would go past, then later the log train would go to Everett with logs and come back with empty log cars in the afternoon.

In the 1940s the engines were steam; later into the 1950s they became mostly diesel/electric. No matter what the source of locomotion, they were all very loud as they passed so closely to our house. We knew most of the engineers and brakemen, and many times they would throw candy to us when going past. When Dad had the smokehouse going, the train would stop and the men would grab some fish and be on their way again. They always made sure to stop on their way down the grade because it was hard to get going upgrade again. Today the grade is a bike trail from Snoqualmie to Monroe.

My day in the summer usually started by Mom catching me leaving and saying, "Where do you think you're going?"

"Nowheres," I would answer.

"You stay the hell out of that bum camp, ya hear?!"

I would grin and head up the tracks and into the camp. The camp varied in population between 100 and 250 men. There wasn't any real security, so they could come and go at will. They came from the surrounding cities: Olympia, Tacoma, Seattle and Everett. If you were found on the streets in any of these cities and you didn't have a job, you would soon be on a bus and headed east to Tolt to the state convalescent home. When the bus arrived, the first stop was the infirmary where the men were sobered up, cleaned up and given a set of clothes. The clothes were almost always a suit and overcoat. I asked my mom once if to be a wino you had to wear a suit, and she explained that when clothes were donated to charity it was usually "Sunday go to

Donna, Dale, Larry

meetin'" clothes and that is what the bums got when they came to camp—some dead man's Sunday suit.

The first person the men met when they arrived was Doc Johnson. Doc wasn't a real medical doctor; I think he was a medic in the military. But at the bum camp he passed out pills and sewed 'em up if they needed it.

Doc

Doc and I became good friends. As mentioned, my dad ran a trapline, and I learned to skin and gut small animals very early in life. Doc had a single-shot .22-caliber rifle that he would let me shoot every now and again. I wanted that gun and he knew it. He had bought it new from Sears & Roebuck for $6, including a cleaning rod and barrel brush.

Doc had his living quarters at the infirmary and he had a few chickens and rabbits in pens next to that. He was well on his way to getting drunk one morning when he said to me, "If you kill and dress those rabbits you can have that gun." Well, I dressed those eight rabbits in record time and had him write a note so that my dad would know that we had a done deal. Sixty years later I still have that little Sears Remington single-shot .22 rifle by my bed.

Doc was a con artist if ever I knew one, and he was always working a deal. One time he told me, "Dale, wine is like poison for these bums. On paydays it would be good if you would watch them when they come back from town to see where they hide their wine bottles and bring them to me. You'd be doing a good thing."

Larry and I would hide in the bushes along the road into camp and watch about fifty wine bottles being hidden over the course of the day. Later, we'd gather them all up and take them to the good doctor. He would lock them up in a cabinet and then sell them back to the bums. We caught him at this and were able to pick up a little spending money on paydays ourselves. This went on for several years. The bums were always coming and going and wouldn't get wise because most of them would be so drunk they wouldn't remember where they had hidden the bottles in the first place.

The camp had a kitchen and diningroom. Meals were served military style and were better than you would imagine. They had roast beef two or three times a week. The kitchen had a walk-in cooler and cutting room where I first learned how to bust down a quarter of beef. The boiler room was a meeting place, nice and warm, just off from the ovens where all the baking was done. The bread dough would rise in pans like small mountains, waiting to be cinnamon rolls and twists. That was one of my favorite places to be.

All of the men had a job to do, not unlike a military base. They worked in the carpentry shop, steel shop or laundry mat, and some were groundskeepers. For most of them, camp jobs were only a couple hours a day and they could take odd jobs outside the camp.

Injuries were quite common, and I would usually run ahead and inform Doc that they were bringing someone in to be fixed up. I remember one guy that would cut his wrists every now and then, more for the attention than to really kill himself. It was never bad enough to actually kill him but it would always be a bloody mess and Doc was

Our family holds the record for the most graduates from Tolt High School, all eight of us. And all five boys (above) were awarded the state electrician award from the FFA (Future Farmers of America). From left to right: Steve, Wayne, Joe, Dale, Larry, Dad.

Yes, eight is enough! From left to right: Wayne, Marcia, Nancy, Larry, Mom, Dad, Joe, Donna, Dale and Steve.

21

Muskrat and bobcat pelts.

getting tired of it. I came running in one day to tell Doc that they were bringing in "Dumbshit," not his real name but one given to him by Doc. I said that he had cut his wrists again and was bleeding all over the place. Doc took charge and started shouting orders, "Put him on that cot in the corner! Dale, bring in that bucket from outside the door and hold it next to the cot to catch all the blood. This is the third time this son of a bitch has tried to kill himself and we're going to help him. Hold him steady now, boys, and I'll cut his damn throat, and Dale, don't you let any of it spill."

The second time he told me to catch all the blood I thought I saw a twinkle in his eye. Up until that time I really thought we were going to kill this dumb bastard. But as it turned out I didn't need to worry about this patient at all. It would've taken ten men to hold him, and I think he set a world record sprinting across camp. The rest of the time Dumbshit was at the camp he never tried to commit suicide again but the name stuck.

Doc Johnson was a stocky, ruddy-faced Swede and was always dressed in whites. When the camp had its Christmas party, Doc played the role of Santa. People would donate toys and things to be fixed up, like bikes and wagons. They would be repaired and painted and at Christmas time in the courtyard they would hand out gifts to needy children in the community. It was kind of a peace offering by the director of the camp for putting up with the winos the rest of the year.

THε Dwarf

Not all the people at camp were winos, some were just misfits. Dwarf was a spastic and if he saw you looking at him he would scream until you left. Usually this worked quite well for him, but I didn't know anything about this.

Sometimes people from town brought clocks and pocket watches to be repaired, and Dwarf was one of the guys who did the fixing. One day I was walking by an open door that was usually closed and looked in to see this very small person sitting at a big, old roll-top desk with clocks all over the place. His arms were above his head and going every which way and his head was shaking back and forth. He had a jeweler's eyepiece in one eye, a pocket watch in one hand and the smallest screwdriver I had ever seen in the other. I slipped inside the door and watched this magic act unfold and in an instant everything came together and the screwdriver found a little screw and removed it and then his head started shaking again and his arms opposing one another all over the place. It was about this time that he saw me and let out the damnedest yell I had ever heard in my life.

I thought he was a little rude but also interesting, so I gave him a smile and sat down on an empty chair and said, "I'm Dale and I've never seen the inside of a watch before. Could I watch you work if I don't touch anything?" Like magic everything came together for him again and he said yes. As the days past we became friends and I would visit him often. He got his parts from old clocks and watches that he would set aside for me to dismantle. I would save the screws and springs and sort them out and stock the little trays and boxes in the old desk. He didn't like to go to the mess hall for meals and the kitchen usually brought his tray to him. I would bring his meals when I could, and he liked that because I knew what food he liked best and would bring him extra helpings of his favorites. He was little in size, but big on desserts.

One day he reached out with a paper match and took some wax out of my ear. I thought my ears must be dirty, but he took the wax and put it on a pivot pin in the spring of a pocket watch. "Wow," I thought, "that's a good thing to know." Who would've thought that earwax was good grease? A day or so later my mother said I needed to take a bath and to wash my neck and ears really well because they were filthy dirty. I told her that I wouldn't be washing inside my ears because that wax could come in handy and should be left alone in case it was needed. She wasn't buying that and said to clean those ears out or she'd do it for me. So I did because I thought the wax comes back on its own and you have it with you all the time anyway.

It was difficult for him to speak, but I found that we really didn't need to and he always seemed happy to see me. About all I learned about him was that he had a twin sister, also a little person, with the same unique features as him.

Dutch Stew

Dutch Van Der Winder lived at the bum camp and had two companions, a guy called Two Gun and a German shepherd named Prince. We had a small farm and Dutch was kind of a hired hand. We raised pigs and Dutch would bring five-gallon pails of kitchen waste from the camp for the pigs, sometimes twice a day. He really had a way with animals and they would follow him around with devotion. Dutch was a good guy but a hopeless alcoholic. If he couldn't find anything else to drink he would mix skimmed milk and gasoline. One time Mom spied smoke below the barn and sent Dad to see what it was all about. Old Dutch and Two Gun (I don't know how he got the name) had gotten drunk so they were kicked out of camp. They raided our garden of vegetables and they had found the carcasses of some mink and muskrat that Dad had skinned and they made a big pot of stew. They had put the muskrat in whole with the tails sticking out of the top of the pot. Every now and then Dutch would stir the stew by the tails.

Der Dutchman's Muskrat Stew
Serves 3 or 4 bums for 2 days

- 2 skinned muskrats — doesn't need to be fresh

- Stolen vegetables — can't always be choosy

- Gut muskrats, leave head and tails on. (Tails will be used for stirring later.)

- Place in pot (does not need to be very clean) with tails hanging over side and bring to a boil.

- Stir every now and again by gathering the tails in hand and giving a good swirl.

- Cook until done and serve when guest is hungry enough or drunk enough to eat it.

- Best served with 6 or 7 bottles of really cheap wine or paint thinner and skimmed milk mixed in even proportions. (Skimmed milk could be substituted with Carnation canned milk.)

Dutch could be a real con also. Once he asked my mom, "Do you ever order from Sears?"

Mom replied, "I do it all the time. Was there something you needed?"

"Yes, I need five gallons of paint thinner. The restrooms and showers at the camp are all dirty and I'm going to clean them and repaint."

So Mom placed the order for him. Dutch checked every day until the order came in, saying that he was very anxious to get going on the project. A few days after the order came there was a knock on the door by Lopez, the camp director. "Mrs. Davidson, did you happen to place an order for Dutch for some paint thinner?"

"Well, yes! He wanted to paint the restrooms. He said they really needed it."

Lopez said, "Well, now they really do need it. They drank all that paint thinner and shit all over the place. Mrs. Davidson I know that you only wanted to help, but it would be best if you never listened to that damn Dutchman again."

Mom and Dutch were still friends but she never ordered anymore paint thinner.

One time Dutch went missing for a few days, but his dog Prince would show up at mealtime so Lopez figured that Dutch wasn't far off and probably up to no good. One evening Lopez told Prince to go find Dutch. The dog took off wagging his tail and led them to Dutch's new winery, where he was busy putting the product into bottles. It was a sad sight to see Dutch walking up the road with Prince slinking along ten feet behind him. Every now and again Dutch would turn around and call poor Prince a traitor or a stool pigeon.

My Dog Mickey

On our little farm it seemed like something was being born all the time—cows calving, horses foaling, pigs farrowing, dogs whelping, rabbits and barn cats having litters, too. At the time it seemed a bit messy, but soon a furry little pup would be licking your face with their distinctive puppy smell and their little puppy breath. To me, out of all the things being brought into the world, the dumb chickens had, by far, the best method. The egg with its neat shape would just pop out, no big deal. And when they got a dozen or so, an old hen would just decide to sit there for a few weeks and the eggs would start peeping. A little chicken would bust out to the delight of the old hen that would be clucking all over like she was the very first one to ever have a hatching. I remember one hatching when there were three red ones, four black ones and three white chicks. Obviously more than one hen had contributed to the nest.

Our dog at the time was Mickey. She was a black Springer spaniel that had been spayed. She loved anything that was a baby, but she was particularly fond of chicks. She could corral some in her front legs and paws and gently nuzzle them. I'd come along and she would let me feel their little fuzziness on my face, too, and soon let them go back to the old hen.

Larry and Dale with our dog, who loved all baby anythings, Mickey.

Raising pigs was a lot of work, but they worked for you, too. The lower part of our property was composed of swamp and blackberry bushes, and the pigs would root out, eat the roots and fertilize as they cleared the land. We had several large old brood sows, all of which we had named. Some were named after flowers: Sweet Pea, Petunia and Daisy May, and some were named after women who Dutch was fond enough of to name a sow after, such as Ruby, Rosie and Liz. The biggest, and by far the meanest, we just called "Old Bitch." On the day a sow had a short visit with the boar, Dad or Dutch would pick one of us kids, mark our thumbnail across the base and tell us that when it grew out that would be when the sow would deliver her piglets.

On the farm when everything was being born, Mom was also keeping up with the program. There were eight of us in the family, three girls and five boys. When the television show *Eight is Enough* was on, Mom used to say, "YES! Eight is enough!" Mom and Dad used to tell people that it was the fault of the late train that would go by and shake them awake and that lots of times (at least eight) they couldn't go back to sleep. But large families were common then. Our family holds the record for the most graduates from Tolt High School, all eight of us. And all five boys were awarded the state electrician award from the FFA (Future Farmers of America).

Raging Bull

The saying, "If March comes in like a lamb, it will go out like a lion," or vice versa, is true for western Washington. It is not uncommon to have winds of sixty to seventy miles per hour in late February to the middle of April. It was one of these very windy days that turned out to be a day that Donna, Larry and I would never forget. The wind was blowing limbs and stuff all over the place, and Mom made the three of us stay indoors and watch out the livingroom window. The neighbor next door had a huge red Holstein bull chained to an iron stake that was driven into the ground. The bull was very mean and had a double ring in its nose; the chain went through the rings and fastened tight around the base of his stubby horns.

A large sheet of aluminum siding had been ripped off the barn and it was being blown about like a tumbleweed. This had the bull's attention, and whenever it got close he would bellow and prance around. The wind would change directions and the distance would widen so the bull would relax a little. Suddenly, a big gust of wind caught the metal and sent it flying at the bull. He lunged and the chain broke

and ripped the rings out of the bull's nose. The chain left was about three feet in length and when he would run it would tangle his front legs and trip him and drive his already bloodied nose into the ground and he would bellow with rage. With a mighty charge he gorged the siding and took it right through the neighbor's fence, across the county road and through our fence and into our field.

In the corner of our field next to the railroad tracks, we had an old white shed built on skids so Dad could move it with the tractor. We used it to house chickens or pigs or whatever needed a house. It was vacant at this time and Dad had moved it into the corner to be out of the way. The door was unlatched and the wind would blow it open then slam it shut with a bang. This little white shed was challenging the bull like a matador with his cape and the bull, full of rage, charged. He went right through the door and was stuck half in and half out of the shed. Around and around in circles they went, then through another fence and the fight ended in the middle of the railroad tracks with the bull standing on a pile of splintered lumber.

This fight had no sooner ended when we heard the whistle of the next challenge coming down the grade—the daily log train heading for Everett. The engineer saw the bull in the tracks and was spending a lot of steam on the whistle and out the release valves on the drive cylinders in a failed attempt to scare the bull off the tracks. The bull accepted the challenge and charged the train. The engine had a cow-catcher front end and the bull hit this at full speed and it slid up and off to the other side of the train out of our sight. For a minute we thought that he had not been run over. Then we saw about four or five cars back that he was being tumbled under the train. After the caboose went past, Larry and I ran out to see what we could see and the bull's head with the chain still attached was laying along side of the tracks and the rest of the carcass was scattered a mile down the grade.

Later, Harry Peterson came by and asked if we had seen his bull. We told him that we had sure enough seen it and showed him what was left. That year March had come in gentle enough, but it left like a raging bull. (Note: Over forty years later, in his seventies, Harry Peterson died of injuries he got when a bull crushed him.)

Harry Dixon

When approaching trains passed certain markers they would whistle, usually before road crossings. We would be able to hear them coming several minutes before they got to our house and that would give us warning to check the tracks for kids, cows or drunken bums. Many times we would check the tracks, find a passed out drunk and go get them off the tracks.

One day I checked and told my brother Larry, "There's a bum on the tracks and I just heard the whistle."

"You should go kick him and wake him up," he said.

Well, after kicking him a few times, I still wasn't getting anywhere. I went back into the garage and told Larry, "I can't wake him and the train is at the trestle." Larry and I ran up to the tracks together, grabbed his jacket and pulled him off the tracks just before the train got there. Then I walked in to the camp and told some fellows to come and get him.

As time went on, there were a few more drunks on the

tracks who we would wake up or pull off before the train smashed them. So when a letter came with a $10 bill for Larry and I for saving a guy's life, we didn't know who had sent it. It seems that one of the guys who Larry and I had pulled off the tracks didn't drink at all and was working at the camp. He was out for a walk on the tracks and had suffered a heart attack. And that was how we met Harry Dixon.

We became good friends with Harry, and he was always making us something. He made us each an Apache flat bow and arrows. It was quite a project. He steamed the wood inside a pipe with steam from the boiler room and with a pipe bender. At the plumbing shop he steamed the yew wood to have a curved shape, then he carved them by hand with hand planers. I could shoot an arrow through the barn walls with it. I had thought that it would stick in the barn. It went right through the cedar walls.

McDivitt's Turkey Farm

Griffin Creek was also one of my favorite places to be. In the summer we would dam it up and make a swimming hole and spend two hours everyday swimming. We thought that it was open year around for fishing but I learned later in life that there were actual fishing seasons. The railroad trestle was over the creek and it was about sixty feet in height. Downstream was McDivitt's turkey farm with several hundred range turkeys.

Every fisherman knows that the best fishing is just on the other side of the No Trespassing sign. If you watch turkeys you will soon know that there is a boss turkey. All the others are busy being turkeys but the boss is always watching, and when you try fishing beyond the sign he will come up to you and make a lot of noise and rat you out. Then the rest of the turkeys join in and, next thing you know, the farmer arrives, too.

One day I came up with a plan to avoid the usual scene when I was on my way to fish, and it involved my bow and arrow. I snuck up to the fence with my bow and arrow, let the boss turkey see me and, just like I had figured, here he came all puffed up and strutting. Damn, he was making this easy. I pulled back part way because he was within five feet and I didn't want the arrow to go through him. I let go and there was a hollow thunk. It hit him square and he rolled over and took off for the farmhouse with all the others chasing him. We couldn't believe our luck and, hell, I had lots of arrows (I didn't mind losing one), so we went fishing and we weren't found out.

A few hours later we were about to sit down to dinner

when there was a knock on the door and Mom went to find farmer John McDivitt holding out an arrow. My mom was just saying, "Thank you, John," when he brought from behind his back a fully dressed Tom turkey, about twenty-four pounds. He finished with, "I found this arrow in my turkey."

Well, my bow and I were separated for a little while, and I went on to develop a better method for silencing turkeys—a ten-foot pole with a wire loop and a pull handle. The turkeys would run right over to the fence and stick their head in the loop. With a quick pull on the handle to close the loop and a little "beep" from the turkey, we could lift a twenty-pounder over the fence with ease. It was quite efficient. And no more of the dying swan ballet performance with my tell-all arrow. Years later, I learned that old John and my dad got a good laugh out of the turkey shooting. John McDivitt could have brought the sheriff and demanded payment but he was a good neighbor and brought a dressed bird instead.

Punch Drunk Boxer

We were always putting nails and coins on the track and as soon as the train passed by we would run out and find these treasures. Flattened nails became little swords and we could give our toy G.I. Joe's a samurai sword and make our own Japanese army. I had an Indian head penny that I carried around that was barely flattened, maybe just a front wheel of the locomotive had run over it. You could still make out the feathers of the headband but the Indian's face looked more like W. C. Fields.

One time we were busy looking for just the right bent nail to put on the tracks when we heard loud talking on the tracks. We peeked out to see this big black man all by himself talking up a storm. He was saying that when he was born he was pure white, like new snow, with pretty hair the color of honey. Then he would jump to the other side of the tracks and question himself, "Well, you're sure as hell black now," jump back to the other side and exclaim, "That's a fact! I was white as skim milk, with golden hair." Larry and I just looked at one another. We had never seen a black man other than in pictures, and we damn sure never met one that was born white and just turned black for no reason. Larry said that he didn't think that it was possible and I wasn't so sure because why would he tell himself that over and over again?

Anyway, the man ran off up the grade fighting somebody that we couldn't see but every now and again he would stop and dance around and fill the air with hard punches. Larry said, "He must think that he's a boxer in a fight, too."

As the days of summer passed, I ran into him here and there, and he was always arguing with himself about being born white. If he saw me watching, he would run after me all the way home and it could be a mile or more. This was wearing heavy on me, and I'd complain to Mom and Dad at the dinner table that the big black boxer chased me home again and Mom would always say, "Well, you must have been staring at him."

"Hell, Ma, I just glanced in his direction and he charged at me like a damn bull or something."

Dad said, "Well, black people don't want you looking at them."

I fell silent while I mulled that over a little and then I said to them all, "I bet it's 'cause he hasn't been black long."

Dad looked up from his plate, a little grin starting to show, and said, "What in the hell ever gave you that idea?"

"He did," I answered. "He tells himself all the time that he was born white as snow and just changed to being black all of a sudden." Larry came to my defense and said that that was so.

Dad just looked at both of us for a bit and then said, "Well then, I really wouldn't be looking at him."

After that little talk it just got worse, and I was fast losing my freeway of childhood. The boxer chased me like a dog chasing a stray cat every damn time we'd meet, sometimes twice a day. This final day he was sitting in the bushes by the tracks at the barn and I was right up to him when he jumped up and gave chase. I went flying in the back door and grabbed my .22 rifle that was just inside the back door. I had to put a round in the single-shot chamber and load it as I ran. The fellow saw me coming, and he started sprinting up the grade. I aimed at the flat of the iron rail and let go the first round. It hit its mark and made that neat noise that all bullets in the western movies make as they hit a rock or something like steel. The carrying off effect of that first shot must have told him, "Yes, it is a gun and it's real and, yes, he is shooting at me," because I never saw anybody run so fast.

Later, when I thought about it, I realized that he could have easily caught me any old time but he just liked to scare the living hell out of this little white kid (probably to see if he'd turn black or something). He didn't chase me anymore and was soon gone. I never saw him again. That evening at dinner Mom told Dad, "The punch drunk boxer chased Dale right to the door and before I could do anything Dale took care of it himself and chased him off with his .22 rifle."

Dad just laughed and said, "The hell he did. Well, that'll probably take care of it."

Sleeping in the Hay

Larry and I had chores to do everyday. We had five or six milk cows that we milked by hand until we were high school age, and then younger brothers took over the job with a milking machine. We also had to put up loose hay into the haymow, and in the winter it was my job to climb up the lad-

Miller 2005

der and fork hay down the opening to the manger below. Over time the hay would become packed down, so a person would have to cut out squares with a big hay knife that had handles and acted as a saw. I would cut about a four-foot square and that would do the morning and evening feeds.

This one morning I climbed up and, to my surprise, there was a big pile of loose hay. All I had to do was fork it down the hole. I figured that Dad must have been up checking on how much hay we had left and he had it cut loose for me. So I grabbed the fork and stabbed it in the pile of hay. That's when all hell broke loose. That pile of hay let out a scream and was shaking the fork right out of my hands. I hit the ladder down in no time and Larry hollered, "What the hell was that noise?"

All I said was, "Run!"

He passed me going to the house and we met Dad halfway to the barn. He was running down to see what the hollering was—it was getting louder by the bloody minute! What Dad found was a bum that had covered himself with hay to stay warm. He was dreaming away when I stabbed him in the ass with a pitchfork. One tine went through his inner thigh and the other tine scratched his testicles. Doc patched him up and told me how close I'd come to making that fellow a steer.

Fussy Old Neighbor

Larry and I also had a job cleaning large chicken houses for a fussy old neighbor. When we got the chicken house all

cleaned out, we would bring in large bales of shavings and scatter them out evenly. The old guy was fussier than any old woman, and he walked around with a wooden ruler and would bend over to make sure that the shavings were exactly seven inches thick. After hours of hard work wheelbarrowing loads of chicken shit, this would get old in a hurry. I'd walk around behind the guy, making faces and turning every now and again to make sure Larry was getting all this humor. Well, he suddenly stopped and bent over to take a measurement just as I had turned to look behind me. I stabbed him right in the ass with this fork I was carrying. The familiar feeling of a live man on the end of my pitchfork returned immediately—and so did the loud screaming.

He tried to tell my folks that I did it on purpose, but Larry told them the whole truth and that it was an accident. Mom called his daughter to find out what his injuries were. There was one tine through the inner thigh and another scratched his testicles. Again I was off the hook, so I didn't have to convince people that I didn't have a fetish about stabbing old guys in the butt with a pitchfork just to hear them yell. Larry and I worked there for a few more years, and we don't think he was quite so particular after he healed up.

Whizzer Motorbike

By the time I reached the age of twelve I pretty well had free run of the camp, and I could come and go as I pleased. I got a Whizzer motorbike from one of the local boys and

41

Dad put a new piston and connecting rod in it so the bike ran as good as new. The tires were only about twenty-six inches in diameter, so it was lower to the ground than an ordinary bike. It would run all day on a tank of gas (about one gallon). I would use it to go fishing and hunting on all the old logging and camp roads. Top speed was about forty miles per hour. And when I was showing off for the bums I always had it wide open, darting all over camp between the barracks and around the dining hall and then running the bases at the softball field. The bums always cheered me on and I'd really put on a performance. Running the bases was encouraged because it kept the base paths free of grass and weeds.

One time I had just finished running the bases and putting on a pretty good show and was making my exit out of camp when I cut a corner of a barracks real close. With the bike almost on its side as I rounded the corner, a pant leg came out of nowhere and my front wheel split the crotch. Next thing I knew, I had picked up a bleary-eyed wino at about thirty-five miles per hour. His eyes were rolling around in his head like marbles in a jug as he hung on to the handle bars while sitting on the front fender breathing bad fumes in my face and yelling that something terrible was happening to him and he was a goner. He was only with me for about fifty feet when the wheel ran up his baggy pants, pulled him under the bike and I rode right over him. I looked back to see if he was a goner and he was crawling real fast for safety of the barracks. All the bums that witnessed this trick riding were hooting and hollering for an encore. But I rode on out of camp like nothing had happened. I didn't ride my Whizzer into camp for a few days, just in case.

Short Pants

Another one of the bums that made a real impression on me was so unusual that he had been given three names: Short Pants, Ole Danny Boy and the Drummer. Whichever name you chose to use, locals knew whom you were talking about, without any doubt. Far too often, we would hear old Short Pants coming out of the camp and past our house on his way down to the state highway. His short pants had once been long ones that he had shagged off at the knee. If it were warm enough this was what he'd be wearing. His drum was a snare drum like those in a drum and bugle marching band with a strap over the shoulder and hanging to one side in front at his waist. Old Short Pants would be stepping lively to the snappy beat of his drum, often singing *Danny Boy*. He had a good tenor voice and it would be going kind of like this:

Oh Danny boy,
rat tat tat the pipes,
the pipes are calling,
rat tat tat,
From glen to glen and down the mountain side.
Rat tat tat,

He would march smartly down to the highway bridge over Griffin Creek, sit on the railing and sing loudly to the more than 1,000 turkeys crowded in close like the hippies were at Woodstock. Griffin Creek is half a mile from our house and we didn't have any trouble hearing his high notes. We knew when he hit a good one when every turkey in attendance gobbled to express his or her pleasure. After the length of time that it takes to drink one or two real cheap bottles of wine, old Short Pants would march back by our house and into the camp. By this time of the day he would be marching to a different beat of the drum, kind of like Porky Pig singing *Danny Boy*:

OH DDDANDANNY BBBBBOY,
tat tap, Glen's calling me,
tat tap, Down the mountain,
tat tap, side,
tat tap, come see me
tat tap, over
tat tap, here
tap tat, in the valley
tat tap, when you come calling
tat tap, bye and bye.

I don't know that anyone has heard *Danny Boy* near as many times as I have. The words would vary quite a bit on the return trip and usually we couldn't wait to share the latest versions with others.

Calf and Buffy

Larry and I were both in 4-H and each of us had a calf that we were leading around and getting tame enough to show at the fairs. By this time, our family had grown by one more and brother Wayne had joined us. He was about three or maybe close to four when the following episode took place.

The folks had gone to town and Larry and I got a good idea that would be fun and help tame the calf that we were

working with at the time. We had stored in the garage the biggest baby buggy ever made. Its wheels were about ten inches in diameter and it had a big, old leather bonnet. We thought that this would be the perfect ride for Wayne to be pulled in slowly around the field by a yearling heifer.

We hitched the rig up soon enough and got the calf to go. However, she started with a jump and the buggy bumped into the cow's rear, another jump and another harder bump in the rear and the race had started. If the race had an announcer, it would have gone something like this, "And they're off. Around the first turn and through the first of several electric fences, the heifer and Wayne ahead by about six lengths." We had a second electric fence to keep the cows out of the ditch. When the calf hit that fence it took on a good electrical charge and let out a bellow and jumped the ditch, the buggy did not. The whole undercarriage was ripped off and left it in the ditch. Now the vehicle that Wayne was riding in looked more like a calf-powered toboggan, and it was skimming across the swamp at record speed. The calf jumped through the three-board fence at the barn and the top board took the bonnet right off, to the delight of Wayne as he squealed with glee.

The training was working quite well and the calf returned right to us, sort of. It got its head stuck in the hand gate and we tackled it and got the remains unhitched. Wayne peeped up and asked, "Can I go again?"

The ride circled thirteen acres in about a minute's time and the folks got home in time to catch us letting the calf go. They just followed the wreckage with their eyes and they could tell what had just taken place. While Dad followed Mom into the house she asked, "What in the hell could they possibly think up to do next?"

Brother Joe

Brother Vernon George Davidson, Jr. joined us next in June of 1947. We call him Joe. There is a short story about Joe when he first learned to talk. He would repeat everything that he would hear. Mom and Dad had just returned from town and were busy getting the groceries out of the car and a bum was staggering on by going into camp. Mom said to Dad (she thought that she was being quiet enough that Joe wouldn't hear), "Look at that nasty old bastard, he pissed all down the front of his pants."

Little Joe yelled, "Hey, you old Bass Turd! Did you pee in your pants?"

Chris Humble

Not all of the men at camp were winos. Some lived there, saved up money and bought land or went to Carnation Farms. I even knew one that got married and worked for the highway department. There was a man that comes to mind that would hang out at camp a lot but I don't know if he was ever a bum or not but he was quite unusual, to say the least. His name was Chris Humble. He bought a few acres out behind the camp for $50 per acre. You could get to his place by going up the Griffin Creek Road and cutting across to the Langlois Road. His place was on the cut road between Langlois and Griffin, later called Humble Road after him.

Everywhere he went, he rode a bicycle and he wore a

leather World War II aviation cap with goggles. He would work a little, but we think he got money from Europe. Dick Langlois was my uncle and used to be the mailman, and he always said Chris got mail from over there and then he'd go to the bank with the letter.

Chris had built a shack on a spring so that he had good water to drink and cold enough to build a spring cooler. He started out with a few goats and some house cats. In about ten years time he had about 150 of each. The goats ate off a hill there and we would refer to it as "Goat Hill." You could be hunting back there and know where the goats were by the smell of them.

Chris and his cats lived off the goat herd. I'd stay for a short visit every two weeks or so but the smell of cat pee, cheese, yogurt and goat would soon get to me and I would remember something that I had to do and get going. The only thing I found that smelled worse than the combination of that place was old Chris himself because he didn't believe in bathing. And if you took a combination of goat cheese, cat pee, Billy goats and old Chris it was powerful. On one visit he was busy with making yogurt and he asked if I would like to try some. "Sure, Chris, I'll give it a try but just a little." Damn. That was awful-tasting stuff, yep, just like Billy goat and cat pee. I found a reason that I had to take off right away and I remember after rinsing the taste out my mouth at the spring behind camp that I decided I wouldn't be eating anything called yogurt anytime soon.

Well, in the last few years I have been coming down with pneumonia. The last bout I had was pretty bad and my wife made me go to our local doctor. Dr. Bob gave me some gorilla strain antibiotics and it knocked me for a loop but it got rid of the pneumonia okay. I didn't know that he'd told Debra, my child bride, to feed me yogurt to get bacteria into me and get me well again.

We got home and I noticed my wife putting these little funny shaped containers in the refrigerator. "What's that?" I asked.

She answered, "Yogurt. Dr. Bob wants you to eat at least two a day for a while."

"Hon, if you go load my .45 long colt pistol and hold it pointed at me I still ain't eating any of that damn stuff." Hell, I started thinking, "How bad could it be to die from pneumonia anyway? It had to be better than eating yogurt."

Debra has her own way of doing things and getting me

past these little hang-ups. It wasn't long until she shoved a spoonful of that stuff in my mouth. It wasn't bad at all and I said, "Are you sure that's yogurt? It's not bad at all."

"What did you think it would taste like?"

"Oh, I don't know...something bad like goat hair and cat pee."

"Really, Dale, I don't know where you get these child-like ideas."

It's been over fifty-five years, so maybe they are working on a better recipe than old Chris had. Every now and again I will eat a little thing of yogurt. Not much taste to it at all. But oh no, I haven't forgotten the taste of that God-awful concoction at Chris Humbles—no, by Jesus, not by a long shot.

Dr.'s Wife

My dad did electrical appliance repair and he had been on a service call at the new doctor's house. At the dinner table that night he was shaking his head and saying, "I met the new doctor's wife and I still can't believe what she was doing."

Ma said, "Oh? Why, what did she do?"

Dad said that he heard a noise in the kitchen and had peeked his head in the door to see what the chirping was about. He said that on the burner, turned on low, was a big, old cast iron skillet with baby ducks running around in it, and it was burning their little feet. She told Dad that she was worried that they were wet and cold. So she thought that she

Miller 2005

could warm them up a little and give them back to the mother that was raising hell out the back door. While shaking her head Ma said, "And I was told that she had a PhD."

I could envision those poor fuzzy, little bastards doing the Mexican hat dance in that hot frying pan. And I didn't know what the hell PHD stood for, but I was positive that it wasn't for Properly Handling Ducklings.

About two miles from their house the Humble Road met up with the Griffin Creek Road. Whenever possible, the logging company would merge the roads and save a lot of wear on the log trucks when they wouldn't have to stop and then go through the gears again. Where Humble meets Griffin Creek Road in the triangle between the roads there is a little clearing in the cedars like an outdoor stage. Sometimes I would come along and the doctor's wife would be out there singing as loud as any fat lady would in the opera, even though she was kind of skinny. She would also, at times, be reading out loud from papers she was holding and saying things like, "Who goeth there?"

I'd say, "It's me, Dale."

Then she might say, "What does thou wanteth with me?"

And I might answer, "Nothin', honest." Then I would tell her that tho had to be getting, and I'd wave goodbye.

Several years later her name came up when a bunch of us were all visiting and the neighbor lady said that the doctor's wife was really involved in the arts and had taught drama classes at the university. I said that I didn't know that.

My mom said, "Oh Dale, don't you remember she used to practice singing and reading Shakespeare out behind camp? What did you think she was doing?"

"Hell", I said, "I just thought she was some lady that liked to talk to herself in the woods."

Mom laughed and said, "And that wasn't a little strange to you then?"

I said, "Ma, think a little on what I might run across on any given day back then and you tell me what would be so different with a lady singing loudly in the woods? Hell, she fit right in with all the other misfits and bums."

My mother laughed and said, "Oh, by Jesus, you are right."

Claude

The property under the trestle at Griffin Creek was owned by the Cunningham's, an old mother and her unmarried son, who was about forty-five years old at the time this story takes place. Claude was a stocky, simple man. He always reminds me of Judd in the movie *Oklahoma*, and the song, "Poor Judd is Dead." Well, so is Claude now, and he damn near went earlier!

One day my cousin Gary and I were picking early apples from the middle of the frame of the railway trestle, and Claude was below cutting old bridge timbers that the railroad had left for him. They burned them in the furnace of their old house for heat. He told us to get out of there and leave his apples be. We figured the tree was on Milwaukee Railroad and the ownership might be in question. He kept hollering, and we were full of apples anyway, so we pretended to leave, and he soon went back to the hard work of hand sawing up those timbers.

On the bridge every forty feet or so hanging on the side were fifty-five-gallon fire barrels filled with rusty, dirty water to fight a fire if one got started. And there were five-gallon buckets to bail the water with. One of these was right above where old Claude was sweating away. We talked it over and decided that being old Claude was so damn generous with his questionable apples that the least we could do was maybe cool him off with a bucket of filthy water from about sixty feet. We snuck out and dipped a bucket and very generously gave it to him. The water hit him with a good force and it flattened him right out. By the time he figured out what hit him we were long gone.

A couple weeks went by and we were in late summer— ninety-degree weather. Gary lived on the other side of the trestle and he walked over to meet me at camp and he said that old Claude was hard at work in this heat and maybe needed cooling off a little. I agreed that it would probably be a neighborly thing to do, and I was still a little peeved about the damn apples growing clear to the top of the tree where he'd never get them because he was scared of heights and wouldn't even walk out on the trestle.

We dipped a big pail of water and just as we were going to dump it the damn bail wire broke off. The five-gallon bucket of water in the pail was heading for Claude and if it would've hit him on the head, it would have killed him for sure. But just as it reached him he bent forward to throw a block of wood in the big pile he had going and the pail glanced off his hip and drove him head first into the wood-pile. When he poked his head up out of that pile like a woodchuck I knew that he was all right and I felt really relieved. He never did see us and I don't think he really knew what made that damn bucket fall at that time, but I'm sure Gary and I were suspected. We didn't do that again because old Claude was a pretty good guy and I didn't want any more accidents.

Old Jim

The neighbor next to Grandma Davidson (where Gary lived) was James McDivitt, unrelated to John the other neighbor who raised turkeys. Jim was a rough-talking old guy, and Gary and I would enjoy spending time with him. One time I kept him in conversation while Gary stole a pack of cigarettes (Old Golds). The next time we came to see him he went to the cupboard and grabbed two packs and threw them to us and said, "You little bastards don't have to pretend to visit me just to steal cigarettes. Now go ahead and light up and we will have a real visit and next time you want some smokes you can do chores and earn them. Now then Dale, how are your grandparents?"

Jim had an old team of workhorses and we would brush them down good and clean out the stalls and he would give us Chesterfields to smoke. He said that he could keep track of how many packs that he was giving us and that Old Golds were too strong for a kid. Next to Jim's old barn was a large brick silo. It had a roof and a ladder both on the inside and on the outside. It was over thirty feet high and it was a good lookout. At the bottom it had an opening about two-foot square and just inside there was a platform over the opening so you could shovel out the bottom when it was full; however, it hadn't been used in years. It was a place where we could smoke and hang out and it was always dry and warm in there. The smoke would go up and out and would never get smoky. One time I was first in and Gary was following and I had just gotten inside and something jumped on my back and knocked the wind out of me and clawed my back as it exited the opening. I didn't know what it was. Gary had just gotten to his knees and was leaning foreword and a bobcat hit him in the chest, bowling him over backwards. He got a good look at him while it was leaving scratches on his chest. We were both scraped up pretty well and we didn't think we should blame it on the neighbor girl, so we had to give up the secret of one of our favorite places. We would still hang out there, but one of us would climb the outside ladder and look in to make sure there wasn't anything in there before we went in and this paid off real big once when there was a whole family of skunks sleeping inside.

THe WiNe TaSter

It was a very nice day—payday for the bums and wine resale day for Larry and Dale's wine business. As mentioned earlier, we would hide in the bushes and watch the drunks stash their extra bottles, which we would find and resell to them. Sometimes we would watch them hide the bottle that we just sold them and get it and sell it again. Our house was close to the road into camp and after they bought a bottle from us they only had about 200 feet to the gate so there weren't many hiding places. If they took a bottle onto the camp grounds it would be confiscated, so they would always drink it down or hide it.

This particular day we had sold all of the full bottles and only had a half pint of Muscatel that had been opened and a few ounces gone. When we had a bottle that had been opened lots of times we would put it in the center of the road and hide in the bushes and watch the bum find it. They would dance around and shout, "It's my lucky day! Damn near full too! Praise the Lord!"

We had put the bottle in the middle of the road and were just hiding when we saw Old Shit Pants walking bow-legged up the county road toward camp. He must have got kicked out of the tavern again for shitting his pants because you could see that he was packing heat. I told Larry, "Hurry! Grab the bottle and let's piss it full and see if Old Shit Pants will taste it."

We got back in the bushes and had to cover our mouths with a hand to keep from giggling. When Old Stinky spied the sack with the full bottle sticking out he just stopped and started talking to himself, "It must have fallen out of their pocket and they didn't even know it. I'll be damned, looks full too." He just kept walking around the bottle and talking to himself. He looked up and down the road to see if he was being watched and when he didn't see anybody he quickly grabbed the prize. He pulled the bottle out and held it up to the light and exclaimed, "Damn fine color, let's give it a try."

Larry and I were doing everything possible to keep from hooting out loud as he admired our pee. He made an awful face when he got a taste of the cocktail we had made for him and he spit it out saying that it tasted like horse piss. Larry whispered, "He's close."

Old Shit Pants put the cap back on the bottle and put it in the sack and placed it in the road just like it was when he found it and then started for camp. He went only a few feet when he stopped, turned around and come back and pulled the bottle out of the sack and took another drink. He swirled it around in his mouth and swallowed it and smacked his lips and said, "That's not so bad," and he drank it down. He tossed the empty bottle into the brush and went into camp. Larry and I both had a hand over our mouths but it wasn't to keep from laughing. We were both gagging and we never pissed in anymore wine bottles. It had been proven to us that day by Old Shit Pants that the bums would drink anything that had alcohol in it and a little pee wouldn't even slow them down. So what would be the point?

Howdy

"Howdy-do" was how I first met old Howdy. He was

standing at the north corner of our yard and he would touch his hat and lean forward with his howdy-do greeting. That's how he greeted everyone. It wasn't long after he first arrived at camp that I met him on the railroad tracks; after he gave the old howdy-do, he gave me another greeting and opened his overcoat and introduced me to more of himself. I asked him if he had to pee or what, and he just grinned at me. Well, this didn't look right so I reached a marble out of my back pocket and loaded my sling shot that Harry Dixon had made me and I aimed it at Howdy. This worked and he closed the overcoat and went off the other way.

Before long he started standing up to the north corner of the yard and would wait until we would be out in the yard and he opened the old overcoat again. He would appear real excited when he'd see my sister, Donna, and I knew what

58

would be coming so I got ready for him. In the garage facing north, down low to the floor was the knothole that we would use to watch the bums hide their wine. I checked to make sure and found that I could see that whole north corner real good. It was within forty feet.

I had a Red Ryder BB gun, just like the one that the kid in *The Christmas Story* got for Christmas. I would shoot a can with it and it would dent it good enough. But if I put a drop of three-and-one oil in the barrel, the BB would shoot right through the can. Earwax wouldn't work on this job; it had to be three-and-one oil. I put a good drop of oil in the old Daisy and sat down to wait. I had a lot of patience for a kid I guess but some things just seem worth it, and this turned out to be one of those times. I didn't have to wait long and Donna only walked by once when old Howdy performed his dastardly deed. I had a good aim and he had the target hanging there and I pulled the trigger.

Do you remember in the western movies when the Indians would dance around the fire the night before they would go on the warpath? Well, old Howdy was doing that dance real good holding himself with both hands and bent forward hopping from one foot to the other all the time yelling, "Yeowheee!!" I was convinced that I got him right on the target. As soon as he could, he went up the road and I could see he was still checking himself out. He didn't open his overcoat at our house anymore. In fact, when he did walk by he would be holding that overcoat closed good and tight. It didn't completely cure him though. He'd be down at the state highway waiting for a car with just ladies so that he could do his little performance. And if they did go into camp to report him it would go something like this:

"What did he look like?"

"Kind of like a dirty bum wearing a suit, brown or gray, I think."

About 235 men fit that description really well. It wasn't long before old Howdy showed his wears at the Grange store to the ladies working there. These gals were raised on farms and they caught him and were beating the holy hell out of old Howdy when the cop come and hauled him off. I saw him once after that walking down 1st Avenue in Seattle when we were on a trip to Penny's and Sears. It looked like the same old overcoat.

After telling this story, I think I should clear up a couple of things about my safety around these old bums and mention that there weren't many like Howdy.

Prince

Remember me saying that old Dutch had a special way with animals? Well, the first few times that I went into camp alone I'd soon find Dutch and his big German shepherd, Prince. Mom says that Dutch was showing Prince my perimeters and, yes, I could go anywhere Prince let me go. The latrines were off limits and he would just kind of block your way and I never ever went in one.

Prince was the police force of that camp. If a couple of bums started arguing loud, old Prince would stick his nose into it, and if they continued arguing it would be in whispers. He would break up a fight in a minute with flashing, snapping teeth and they had better stop or before long it was two bums with bad dog bites on the way to see Doc Johnson.

One day a new bum arrived, and when Prince went over to smell him, the new bum went to hit Prince with his cane. He was soon flat on his back with Prince on his chest showing him his teeth like he was saying, "Look what big teeth I have," and all the bums sitting around on the many benches cheered and laughed. Then Dutch rescued the new arrival with "Don't ever try hitting that dog again, 'cause I ain't always around to save you. He won't bite anybody except those that need it."

He truly was a prince of a dog, and I really loved him. I always had my own dog but ours were taught to stay at home and couldn't go into camp because Prince had a job to do and he wouldn't leave except with Dutch. When I would leave he would see me off the property and then high tail it back to one of his many posts where he kept an eye on things. Mom says Dutch trained Prince to be my guardian and I would agree.

Dad

I already mentioned that my dad ran a trapline and that he was in good physical shape. He was just six feet tall and weighed 185 to 195 pounds. Out behind camp, as we used to say a lot to describe the area, was Weyerhaeuser Timber company land. The headwaters of the Tolt River and the fork in the river were about twenty miles from our house. Some time around 1960 the city of Seattle built a dam on the south fork. I am sure that the city didn't have a permit from King County because in the 1970s a building inspec-

Dad with us three, Larry, Dale and Donna, 1942.

tor came to our sawmill and asked Wayne and I if we had a building permit for the mill and what year was it issued. I said it would be easy for him to find because we used the same damn permit that Seattle used when they built the dam. We never heard from them again.

Right below that damn dam is a big, old fir windfall reaching across the south fork of the river and Dad would use this log bridge to get to the ridge on the other side of the river. He shot a big, old Pacific blacktail four-point buck. Dressed, it turned to be about 180 pounds. With head and hide on, he packed the deer on his back across the foot log and home. We, my brothers and I, have measured the mileage to the log from our house. It is right at seventeen miles. Now back in Tennessee, where my old buddy Franklin Turner lives, that same buck would be a ten point, not that old Franklin lies so much. It's because they count every point on the rack, eye guards and all.

When I was about four years old, Larry, six, and Donna, eight, Mom and Dad would leave Donna in charge and they would go to the barn to milk the cows and feed the other animals. The barn was about 200 feet from the house. They had been gone but a short time, when a drunken bum tried to get in the front door. Donna bravely ran to the back door and called for Dad. The bum came to the back door and tried to get in that way, yelling and shaking the door. Donna went to the front door and yelled again; Dad heard her that time and came on a dead-out run. Dad and the bum met at the corner of the house and Dad hit him with a straight right to the chin and knocked him out cold. He grabbed him up put him over his shoulder and he lit for the camp with mean-ingful strides to the courtyard were there were always bums sitting around on benches.

Dad dropped him to the ground and stated, "This son of a bitch just tried to break into my house with my kids inside. When he comes around you tell him and anyone else, next time somebody is going to be dead."

There was a choir of voices, one saying, "You're right Vern, can't be no trespassing," and another spoke up and said, "Scaring the kids, too, the damn fool." There was no next time.

Every now and again Dad would hand Larry and I a box of ammo for our rifles and tell us to go shoot some. He said it would improve our aim and let the neighborhood know we have guns and we can still afford to buy bullets.

DONE HUNG HISSELF

I don't know how often a wino needs to take a drink, but I think if they had a bottle hidden that they would visit it often. We had a steady flow of bums walking just outside camp and around our house from both directions. Larry and I would follow often and find everything that they dropped, probably when they would pull the sack with the bottle in it. The sack was so that you wouldn't know what was in it. After seeing a lot of bums drinking from a paper sack at least fourteen million times I could never figure out why the hell they didn't just get rid of the sack. Why they didn't is beyond me.

My cohorts and I were always looking for wadded up bills, tobacco, pipes and all kinds of stuff. One time I had

spent the night with my cousin, Gary, just across the railroad trestle and I was headed home to do my chores when
up ahead I spied a new rope tied to the ties and trailing
below. What a find! We were always looking for good ropes
that we could make calf halters out of and damn it if this
didn't look to be brand new. I hurried ahead and knelt down
where I could see where the rope was trailing off to and I
saw a bum. Rope tight around his neck, just barely swaying
back and forth. I don't know what makes a person run from
a dead bum but I was sure as hell puttin' one foot in front of
the other now and I was home in record time. Flying in the
back door I was yelling, "Dad! Come quick! A bum done
hung hisself."

We went back and he was still there and Dad went to
Grandma Davidson's house (his mother's place, where
Gary lived). He rang up the operator to send the coroner.
Dad, Gary and I went back across the trestle and waited for
them to come. It took two hours for the sheriff and the coroner's wagon to get there. The sheriff walked across the trestle to have a look but the old, fat coroner stayed below. He
called up to Dad, "How long do you know that he's been
hanging there?"

Dad answered, "I know of two hours for sure."

The old coroner said, "Well, that's long enough. He's
dead for sure. Cut the rope and let him fall down here."

The sheriff cut the rope and let him fall about thirty feet
to the ground. The bum had hung himself off to the end of
the trestle so it wasn't too far to the ground. I was thankful
for that because it was more than sixty feet in height in the
center. That new rope went with the body. I wasn't interest-
ed in having it anymore anyhow. The sheriff cut the rope
beyond the knot and that short piece of rope tied around the

tie was left there for several years until the railroad rebuilt the bridge.

Hobo

Across the tracks from the barn were a spring and a camp-fire pit with some kettles and cans hanging in the trees. This was the "hobo" camp, made up of transients. Sometimes the bums would be hanging out there when they got kicked out of camp to sober up from a good long drunk. But most of the time it would be a hobo or two having a meal and catching a train east. Once I was watching a hobo boil up some eggs that he got for doing some chores at Amos' chicken farm, which was close by. He had a good boil going on, about one dozen, and when they had cooled he was putting them in his pockets so that he could catch the train that would be coming up the grade soon. It was a long, hard pull for the freight train. Many times it was 100 cars or even more. At our house it would be going slow enough that you could step aboard. I said, "You must not be going far."

"Oh? Why do you think that?"

"Well, a dozen boiled eggs and a couple apples ain't goin' far."

He grinned, held an egg up and said, "Do you see this egg?" I nodded my head yes, and he carried on, "Day after tomorrow I'll be eating this very egg in Chicago, Illinois."

Later that evening I asked Dad if that was possible. He thought about it and said, "Yes, if he catches his train all right. He's probably in Spokane now and it's a nonstop straight shot to the Chicago stock yards."

I was impressed and I stored that information away just in case I ever wanted to see Chicago. Several years later I did go to Chicago but in a 707, and we flew right over those stockyards; that vast railroad yard was something to see from the air. I thought of the hobo and as I closed my eyes and sat back in the seat I could see a certain hobo eating a boiled egg. I've been thinking that I'd like to take the passenger train to Chicago from Seattle and boil up a dozen eggs for the trip. I think I'll mention it to my child bride and see if she would like to see one of the biggest railroad yards in the world. How do I know that it's one of the biggest? Well, the hobo told me almost sixty years ago.

Sunday Tractor Ride

A lot of Sundays we would have company for dinner and my mother would cook up a big feed. We would peel ten pounds of spuds for starters and she would have a big beef or pork roast and sometimes chicken. When chicken was the choice she would tell Larry and I to catch and chop the heads off of the two biggest fryers and she would scald and pick them. She would brag that "them boys always catch and bring me the biggest ones and in record time. I don't know how they do it." It was real easy, actually, and this is how it was done: I told you earlier that Dad was a trapper and that he had at least 100 traps, sizes one through four, and even two bear traps. The smaller the number, the smaller the trap, so we would take a #1 single-spring muskrat trap and hang it on the wall, all set and ready to spring. It was hanging at the height that only the biggest fryer could reach. We would put a little spot of fingernail paint on the trigger plate (chickens can't pass up red because they think it is blood) and they would jump to peck that red spot. The winner was dinner. And that was all there was to that.

It was after one of these Sunday dinners that Larry and I thought that we would take a little ride on the old home-made tractor that my dad had made. Larry was in the third grade and I was in the first. I could hang on pretty well. We went across the tracks at the crossing and drove into camp, made a U-turn and were coming back out when we met old Tom the Russian fixing the road. He would, with a wheelbarrow, haul clinkers (cinders) out of the furnace and smash them with a maul and fill the holes in the road. It worked pretty good and made a good patch.

Tom had everything in the middle of the road and was

Dale and Larry on the Washington State ferry in the San Juan Islands.

waving us to go around. No problem for Larry because he was a good driver and we just went to go around. Well, the road gave way and the tractor rolled over on its top, pinning my brother under it. I was standing up on the tractor when it went and it threw me about twenty feet headfirst into a brush pile. I broke my nose (for the first time, not the last) and both my eyes were soon swollen shut. But my brother was, by far, worse off. I saw Larry under the

Mom, Dad and Dale

tractor with a bolt right through his wrist and his scalp had been peeled back from a sharp, cut-off sapling. I could see his pulse and the bleeding from his head wound.

Old Tom, who wasn't to fault, grabbed hold of that tractor and on the second try lifted it and rolled it off Larry. He only spoke Russian but that didn't mean that he wasn't smart or caring. He gathered my brother as gently as he could and carried him across the tracks and home. Well, we both went to the old hospital that was at Weyerhaeuser Mill Community in Snoqualmie. After they had sewn up Larry and got him in a bed, old Doc Templeton said, "Let me look at your nose, son, I won't hurt you. Not a bit." With his thumb rubbing the side of my bent nose and his fingers cupping my chin he snapped his thumb. Wow! What a noise and a hell of a shot of pain. He turned to Ma and said, "He'll be all right but he's probably going to holler for a while so would you mind taking him out of here?" He was right. I could holler right now just thinking about it.

The head nurse was named Woods, a homely redhead, Katherine Hepburn-type who smoked and would go to the tavern and shoot a good pool stick and put nickels in the pinball machines. She was as rough as they get but a damn good nurse. She knew that I really missed my brother and she bent the rules and let me spend time with Larry when mom went shopping.

Larry could read well and Mom had bought him a book, so I got in bed with him, dirty shoes and all. He was reading *Little Black Sambo* when Woods came in; she made me get out of bed and sit in a chair by the bed. It was okay, I guess, but I nearly lost my brother and I wanted to be as close as I could for a while. Larry ended up staying in the hospital for about two weeks. We both were okay in a little time and soon got back to normal. (I've heard people use that phrase, "back to normal," I ain't sure I know what that means.)

Tom the Russian

I want to tell you a little more about Tom the Russian. His only reason for being at the camp was that he had made it to Seattle after World War II. He was born in Siberia and fighting the Germans when he got a chance to get on a ship that brought him to Seattle. He had no job and couldn't speak English, so off to the bum camp he went. He was a very good man and he worked all the time. When the camp closed and he had nowhere to go good old John McDivitt (remember, the turkey farmer?) let him put up a shack on Griffin Creek and Tom spent the rest of his life living there. Even after John's death, John's daughter built Tom a new house there to live in. They let him keep the old shack for storage and he lived back in it most of the time. The McDivitts were good people. A few years later some local

Tom's shack at McDivitt's on Griffin Creek.

writer wrote about the old Russian, but I don't think they even mentioned the bum camp where I know he spent at least fifteen years.

Shorty

The very first barrack just across the tracks and a few feet into camp was where Shorty lived; he was the camp's night watchman. His end of the barracks was walled off from the rest of the men and the couple of windows were painted black. This was so he could sleep during the day. Right after breakfast old Shorty would go to bed. An hour or so before my bedtime (that would vary between summer and winter) was the time that I could visit Shorty before he went on his rounds and before I had to be in bed. The inside of his place was darker than the inside of a cow so we just sat on the steps and lit up one of our pipes and would have a smoke. On one of my scavenger hunts I had found a darn near new corn cob pipe, and he'd let me fill the bowl from his big can of Prince Albert that he always seemed to have and we would have a little smoke. When I'd come home sometimes Mom would say, "Been over seeing Shorty haven't you?"

I would say, "How did you know, Ma?"

And she'd reply, "I can smell his pipe smoke on your clothes." She didn't know about my pipe, which I kept hidden just inside the old barn.

Shorty wasn't too tall, you could probably guess by now, but he kept a big, healthy handlebar mustache. He would say, "When I was in the force..." or "When I was part of the force..." I don't know what he meant or where the force was. He had a .38 short-barrel (naturally) Colt police special and he would say, "I carried that when I was active." He also had a 16-gauge Stevens single-shot shotgun that kept standing in the corner inside the door.

Shorty only left camp about two times a month and he would ride into Tolt in the station wagon with Lopez, the camp director, to get his groceries. Shorty had a real little cook stove, and sometimes I'd have a cup of his "joe." It would be in a tin cup and he'd serve it at about 2,000 degrees. Lots of times I'd visit for an hour or more before I could drink that damn stuff. He would put a little whiskey in his and drink it right down. I didn't see how that little bit of booze could cool it off, but he could sure drink it hot.

Shorty's duty rounds of the camp were mainly to watch for fire, and it was proven necessary. Many times over he would catch a fire in time before it did real damage. Old Shorty would walk around a little taller for a couple days (even though he was still about a foot shorter than the average parking meter). He kept watch on the boiler all night and kept the black bear out of camp with a shot in the butt with the 16-gauge and birdshot. The camp had a garbage dump right beyond the baseball field and you could go look at a black bear most anytime.

Shorty would change his schedule sometimes when there was going to be a big deal baseball (softball) game. Old Short was a damn good catcher, I think because he was already kind of low to the ground. He could hit and run, too! I can hear all the cheering yet today when he'd come to bat. "Come on, Short! Get a hit, Short!" And he would usually do just that.

The Bum Camp is Closing

Well, it had been in the local paper, "Bum Camp Closing." It was a sad time for old Short and me. It was 1951, the bums were already starting to leave and you could see the number going down. Sitting smoking on the steps I'd ask old Shorty, "What are you going to do? Can you stay?" "Nope," he'd answer, and he didn't want to talk about it so we just sat and smoked some of old Albert. I tried to let go of it, his leaving and all.

Eventually the day did come, and he pulled his big old watch out to check the time so he could start the shift. I had seen him do this a thousand times, only this time he undid the chain and handed that old timepiece to me. I knew the watch very well and my other little buddy, the watch repair specialist, kept it in real good working order. I started to hand it back and I'd commented that it sure was a good one and he said, "It's yours, take it."

"Shorty, how in the hell are you going to know when to get up if you don't have your watch?"

"There won't be a shift after tonight anyway. Take it, Dale, damn it. I want you to have it. Now get for home."

He turned and walked away and left me looking at him leave on his way for the boiler house. I went home and got in bed and held old Shorty's watch while I slept.

When I woke up I heard my parents talking with a neighbor and Mom said, "Oh, Dale's up. Did you see Shorty last night?"

"Yeah, for a little while. Why?"

"Well, sometime early this morning they found him dead. They think that he'd shot hisself."

It took a while before I told them about the watch and I showed them. They got real worried and said that it had to go back. It was decided that it should go to old Lopez because Shorty's death was still under investigation and his watch being missing would be suspicious. So, I gave up the watch.

There were a few people that still thought I'd go around stabbing old guys in the ass with a pitchfork just to hear them holler, so I guess they'd say that I'd shoot one, too, just for his watch. When you are young and hurting bad inside, you don't always reason real well. I know now that I should've just kept it for old Shorty, just like he asked me to. I could've hidden it with my corn cob pipe and nobody would have been wise to it.

At the time of this writing, our daughter, April Jones, is about to give life to her second child and my twelfth grand-child. It is already known for sure that this one is a boy. The parents have already picked out a name, but I think Shorty Jones could be a good nickname. Yep, just kind of rolls off the tongue—Shorty Jones.

Dad with winter steelhead.

Part II
Stories from the Farm

Dad's Plum Tree

I think that one of the things I like most about living in Washington State are the four distinct seasons. I love all of them equally and find myself looking for the telltale signs of the approaching change.

The fall harvest included hunting and fishing, and I would look forward to spending extra time with my dad fishing for salmon and steelhead to be put up for winter. The smokehouse would be full and going all the time, hams hanging at the top and bacon slabs to be cured slower on the top racks. Then there'd be the fish on the lower racks, a little closer to the heat. The fish would rotate out in a 24-hour period and it wouldn't take long to smoke a few dozen—the Davidson daily limit. Sea-run cutthroat trout would follow the salmon up the river and I would always be pestering Dad to go and catch some. They would run in size from twelve to twenty-two inches, weighing up to four pounds, and put up a good fight on light rigging.

Dale in the front yard of the place he and first wife Arlene built. A pond is in the background and home place up the hill.

Dale with his horses Babe and Pawney.

Picture with white tail deer at brother Larry's ranch in Colville. Left to right: Dad, Steve, Joe and Dale.

Deer in pickup. Left to right: Dale, Steve and Dad, also at Larry and Elaine's ranch in Colville.

The mouth of Griffin Creek where it met the Snoqualmie River wasn't far from our house, and we could just put a row boat in at Pleasant Hill farm and drift down and fish the mouth of the creek then drift another mile or so to where we would have the pickup truck waiting. I remember this one time when dad said that if I would help him pick plums at the old homestead, he would take me fishing. I agreed and off we went. Right on the riverbank there was an old orchard; Dad had picked yellow plums off the same tree when he was a kid, and he was quite fond of them. The river had changed course years earlier and cut through the orchard and every high water it would cut a little more and Dad must have known that his favorite plum tree didn't have long. We caught several fish and I keep thinking that it would soon be time to pick plums and keep my promise. We drifted around the bend in the river and the plum tree loaded with plums was laying over the river only about three feet from touching the water. Dad guided the boat in under the tree and grabbed a hold on it and started shaking it real hard. The boat was full of ripe yellow plums in about thirty seconds and he said, "What do you think Dale, have we picked enough?" I thought that we had plenty, and I didn't mind that kind of picking at all. The next high water took Dad's favorite plum tree, but the last harvest was a dandy.

Deer Hunting

We hunted deer for the meat and it was serious business, and dad was a good teacher. We were taught at a very young

Diana, Darryl, Douglas, and Duane in front of '67 Ford pickup.

Grandma Weber, first wife, Arlene, Dale, and Grandma Davidson, just months before she went missing.

age to respect and treat all guns as if they were loaded and never bring one in the house without the breach being open and fully unloaded. I shot my first legal deer when I was twelve years old. I was with my dad carrying an empty 30-30 Marlin rifle, and the box of shells was in Dad's back pocket. We came upon two bucks about fifty yards from us and Dad handed me a shell and said, "Take the one on the left, it looks to be a little heavier and you should be able to shoot it in the head." I didn't have any trouble hitting it in the head and over the years I have shot many more, usually in the head. My brothers and I have bagged everything that is legal and some things that ain't; however; I quit hunting a few years ago and about the only thing that I shoot now is the breeze.

I heard my father say once, "Dale is the best hunter that I have ever known." This was a real compliment from the best friend that I ever had. He only told me that he loved me twice—once when he was drunk and once when he was near death. His father never showed him nor told him that he loved him. I think that that was the reason Dad couldn't say that he loved me, but he showed it to me many times over.

Grandma Davidson Went Missing

On June 14, 1958, Grandma Davidson went missing. She was eighty-three years old. Dad and I felt that she wandered off and that she was close by and all of us started searching for her. The news media and the sheriff depart-

Dale and Dad's old Chev pickup in the background.

ment would report sightings in Issaquah and Snoqualmie and we would be side tracked. On July 14, a fisherman found her lying face down in the creek about a mile and a half up the creek in very heavy underbrush. Dad and I had searched to within 100 feet of the site when I turned back and told Dad that I didn't think an eighty-three-year-old could go past that point. We'd come that close the first day to finding her.

The coroner's report stated that she had a heart attack and fell into the stream and had water in her lungs; they ruled that she had more than likely drowned. I was taking this as a failure on my part for not finding her and that she died out in the woods alone. Dad and I were sitting on the log that she was sitting on when she had the heart attack and he said, "Look around you at the peaceful beauty and listen to the babble of the stream and tell me, isn't it better to have died here then being keep alive in a nursing home?" I felt okay after that and I don't feel any blame today. My father relieved me of that on the 15th of July, 1958.

Expelled from High School

Just on the other side of the trestle, over to the east, the railroad owned forty acres. The property was a hill that the grade cut through and was held in reserve for its gravel. Every now and again Milwaukee Railroad would use the siding and a big shovel would load out several ore cars with gravel. The top of the hill was flat and heavy in growth of good timber. Milwaukee wanted the property to be logged off and they sent their timber cruiser to estimate the amount of marketable timber. The estimate was right at 200,000 board feet. Pa said, "There's a hell of a lot more wood than that on that hill." So we bought the timber rights at 200,000 board feet and in the next year Dad, Larry and I took out 430,000 board feet, and we didn't clearcut it either.

In 1954 Larry was a junior and I was a freshman. After school we would go straight home and go up on the hill and fell and buck fir trees into logs to be hauled to Davis Mill just four miles away on the other side of town (Tolt/Carnation). I liked most of the teachers, with the exception of maybe one. He was a retired air force captain and Tolt High was his first teaching position as a typing and journalist Nazi. He let all of us white trash know that he wouldn't be moving to our cow shit town and our hick high school was just a temporary beginning for him.

I had typing in third period. When I got to my typewriter a gal was just finishing a paper and said, "Hi, Dale, I am almost done."

I said, "Hey, I ain't going nowhere, take your time."

I turned to find the teacher yelling into my face to sit down. I looked around at all the seats taken and said, "Where do you expect me to sit?"

He grabbed the front of my shirt in a fist and said, "I don't give a damn if you have to sit on the floor."

I didn't think that I hit him that hard, but he went backwards through the open door and sat his ass on the floor, just like he told me to do. The office gave me fifteen minutes to be clear of the school property and I went home and changed into my work clothes and Ma said, "Pa's felling. You had better get up on the hill and get to work." I heard his saw on the south end so I went to the north end and started my saw. The distance that I put between us wasn't entirely for safety reasons. I knew Pa was going to be pissed and I wasn't ready to confront him with it.

Well, he heard my saw and when I finished a cut I looked up to see him sitting on a stump and he said, "Home a little early ain't ya?"

I said, "Yeah, they asked me to leave a little early," and I told him the whole story.

When I finished, he looked at me hard and asked, "Dale, are you telling me the truth?"

I said, "Yes, Pa, it's the truth. And several of my classmates seen the whole thing."

He said, "Don't worry a bit. You'll be in that damn school in the morning."

He went and jumped into the old Chevy pickup and took off down the hill. The high school was about two miles away. Up on the hill where I was, I could hear him finding all the gears with the gas to the floorboards all the way and the screech of the tires when he got it stopped. About ten minutes went by and I heard him fire up and come roaring back up the hill. I was thinking that he should be showing up when I heard his saw start and he went to cutting over on his side. I couldn't stand it anymore, so I walked over and sat on a stump and waited for him to finish the cut. He saw me, so he shut of his saw, came over, sat down by me and said, "Dale, we'll get you in again next year for sure."

I asked, "What happened? Wouldn't the principal listen to ya?"

He said, "Nope, and he shoved me and told me to get the hell off the property, and I knocked him on his ass."

The typing teacher never came back to school to teach.

He said that I should have to pay for his dental work but it was found out he got it free on base anyway. It was said that the school board had a paper signed by about 200 students that had seen the whole thing firsthand and swore that the teacher had hit me first. (Tolt High's enrollment at the time was about ninety-three.)

Receiving my Diploma

I worked that summer, 1955, at Davis Sawmill located about two miles north of Tolt. I was mostly working on the green chain. (When logs are being sawed, the lumber comes out on a moving chain to be sorted to size, i.e., 2 x 4, 2 x 6, etc. The lumber is fresh and called green, hence the name green chain.) They were cutting railroad ties and it was my job to pull and stack ties all day. My grandpa, Gilbert Boersma, wanted me to go back to school, and he bribed me with the offer of a new 30-30 Winchester carbine rifle if I would graduate from high school. He really didn't have to make the offer because with working at the mill all week and the woods on weekends, going back to school was winning out. At my graduation, out in the crowd was a grinning old farmer with a suit jacket on over a new pair of bib overalls sitting there with a spanking new Winchester rifle. When they called out my name to come and receive my diploma, up came my Grandpa Boersma and a big cheer went up as I got a big hug. I took my seat with my diploma in one hand and my new rifle in the other. Oh, by Jesus, 'twas nineteen fifty and sebben'.

Tanning with the Hair On

Steelhead fishing was an important part of our early life, and my brothers and cousin Gary fished every river in the state that had a run in it. My dad was the teacher and well-known for catching both summer and winter run. Steelhead return to spawn, like salmon, but they don't die and most go back to the sea and then return again. The flesh is more pink than a salmon, and I think they are a better flavor, although, I like all salmon (except chums, too damn fishy). I had, in the past, free access to Carnation Farms property and I could come and go as I wanted. I kept the coyote population in check for them and they were very grateful that I could keep their losses down.

One weekend I shot thirteen adult all in prime pelts. I would freeze the pelts and when I had two dozen or so, I would take them to the tanner in Marysville and he would tan the pelts, with the hair on. I would sell these to a furrier in Seattle to make ladies' long coats. They only used a strip about four inches wide from the center of the pelt and it would take thirty pelts to make one coat.

One year, the old guy in Marysville died and I needed to find a new tanner because I had a freezer full of pelts. So I let my fingers do the walking and turned to the yellow pages. Right over in Issaquah the ad said, "Now open seven days a week tanning." I got a young lady on the phone and I asked her if they could tan with the hair on. She laughed and replied that they could.

I said, "Good, I've got thirty or forty coyotes. Can I bring them right over?"

She said, "Good God! Are they real?"

I said, "Hell yeah they're real, but dead."

She said, "SICK!" and hung up. That was when I learned that they tan people too (with the hair on), but they prefer them to be alive.

New Game Warden

We had a new fish and game warden at the time of this story, and he said in the coffee shop that he knew for a fact that Gary and Dale were going down on the farm property and catching more than the limit of three winter steelhead per day and that in just a matter of time he would be writing us up. One of the used cow salesman that was always present and active with trading and selling to the local farmers heard this statement and soon told me to watch out for him. A short time later, Gary and I were down on Carnation Farms property fishing for winter steelhead. It was in December and colder than the average witch's tit flying north in a hailstorm and we had each caught a fat hen steelhead, full of egg roe that we would later cut up and cure in borax. It would then be used for future bait. (We had a freezer full at all times.)

We agreed that it was time for a coffee break and Gary said that he had a bottle of booze in the truck to warm us up. I looked across the river where I had seen a flash and saw the warden watching us with glasses. I told Gary not to look over and that the warden was watching us. I said, "I will turn and point at him and then we should grab our fish and run like hell for the truck." It worked very well and here he come like a bat out of hell.

He had to go up the river to the bridge to cross and he hit a car when he pulled on the bridge. He just kept going to the farm where he trespassed onto the private farm road and drove right through a wooden gate and broke it all to hell with boards (sawed by Davidson's Sawmill) flying every where. We were watching him come and Gary said, "Geez, I didn't think he'd lose it like this. He drives like a mad man." He skidded to a halt blocking us in and jumped out demanding, "Where's the fish?"

We showed him the fish and licenses and punch cards, and I asked, "What's your problem, other than you can't drive for shit?"

He turned to Gary and said, "He pointed at me and said something to you and then you both ran. WHAT DID HE SAY!?"

Gary calmly said, "He told me to look at the dumb shit new warden spying on us and then he said, 'I'll race you to the truck.'"

Later, the warden claimed that he was in pursuit of some poachers when he sideswiped the car on the bridge but nobody believed that we could have poachers living in our community. The local sawmill (Davidson's, which we built in 1973, about two miles south of Tolt) donated to the Carnation Farm crew some 2 x 6 fir so that they could build a better gate. We got a new warden, too, and this one didn't run around like a "mad man."

Fishing with a Dupont Spinner

In the fifties, we owned twenty acres on the Langlois side of the Tolt River and above Lake Langlois about one mile. We would drive up there and spend many hours swimming in the river. One of the deep holes was full of summer run steelhead and Larry and I thought that a Dupont spinner might work on them. For you nonfishing people, that's Dupont, as in dynamite. Dad always had a box with caps and fuse for shooting stumps, so we helped ourselves. The plan was to tie a stick of powder to a wet piece of wood that would sink and short fuse it, throw it in upstream and get ready to catch the fish below.

Larry threw the charge in, we ran below and waded out waiting for the fishing to begin, when a hell of a blast went off about three feet from us. While we were sitting in the river, we decided that we needed to be a little more sure where the blast should take place. It was agreed that if we tied a stick to a pole that we could crawl out on a log and hold it in the right place when it went off. Turns out that was another bad idea.

When we shoved the loaded pole in the water the fish all took off. Also, we couldn't hold the pole against the current. There was a hell of a blast about three feet directly under us and this time it blew the log and us about four feet into the air and the suspense of not knowing just when the blast would take place shook us up pretty good. I wouldn't recommend this type of fishing to those who fish to relax.

Damn, we needed a better plan. Dad was an electrical contractor at the time and a large part of his business was putting in new larger ampere service panels, so he had in stock four-inch diameter ten-foot length conduit. The plan was to stand the pipe on end and work it into the gravel. The fish got used to it being there and crowded around it; we were ready to go fishing again. Larry fused two sticks and said that should be enough (a hell of an understatement). He told me that he would drop the charge into the top and that I should count to three and pull up on the pipe. The blast took place at the count of two and it felt like my arms had been stretched to where I would be able to slam-dunk a basketball from the foul line.

This bazooka-fired shot of water went about a hundred feet in the air. Larry was already downstream and busier than a one-armed short order cook pitching fish up on the bank for me to catch. I hadn't got used to having arms four feet long and I wasn't catching many but we got all of them and soon had them filleted and in a salt and brown sugar brine to soak overnight. (Brine: one gallon water, one cup of table salt, a half cup brown sugar—very tasty. We used to take smoked fish to school and give it to teachers to improve our grade average.)

It wasn't until the next day when we were filling the trays in the big smokehouse that I noticed the ringing in my ears had gone.

Good Eatin' Bruin

One morning Bob Andrealli, a local farmer, came to our house and said that a big black bear was tearing up the orchards and that they wanted us to come and shoot the bear. A bear that has been getting fat on berries and fruit was usually damn good eating and we thought that we could, at least, take half and give the other half to the farmer. If a bear has been eating the spawning salmon and dining at the local garbage dump they ain't fit to eat and you couldn't stand to smell it cooking.

The orchard was an old one, up on the hill just north of Tolt and big blackberry bushes had grown all around it. My Uncle Bob and brother Wayne were with me and when we got there old Anderson, who owned the orchard, came running and said, "The bugger is to the top of the tree and really raising hell." I told Bob that I would go around to the other side of the tree and come in and shoot the bear out of it. I got around to the other side and found the berry bushes were so high that the only way in was to crawl on my hands and knees and go in the way the bear did. I hoped like hell that Bob didn't scare him so the bear and me would meet face to face in under the bushes.

I have never shot a horse before but I come damn close that day. About half the way in, Anderson's old workhorse smelled me and blew his lips really loud and stamped his big old front foot at the same time. Bob said that I popped my head up out of the briers like brier rabbit. Wayne said, "No, with the briers on his head and the beard I thought that he looked more like Jesus." The bear was still busy breaking down a pear tree and I dropped him with a shot to the head with my 30-30.

Some time later Paul Johnson, dad's fishing buddy, was at the house and mom told him that we were having bear steaks so he had better stay. He said that maybe he would have one but that Annie, Paul's sister, would have dinner ready when he got home. Paul was six feet six inch-

93

Cedar Log Tavern

*Thinking of writing a book,
on a beach on Lopez Island.*

*Home place pond and
Ma's ducks, Tolt.*

es tall and weighed about 285 pounds. He didn't grow that big by being finicky. After he finished the first steak he reached for the huge platter and slid half the steaks off onto his plate and said, "When I'm hunting, there won't be another bruin getting past me in the woods." It was a good-eating bear.

MaN iN Back of a Pickup

In the early sixties, Arlene (my first wife) and I bought an acre of ground from Dad and Mom and built a house. About this same time Larry and Elaine (his only wife) bought five acres up out of Fall City and built a house. Larry's house was on the old road from Fall City to Issaquah and just up the road from him was the backside of the Boeing Farm. With the 'NO TRESSPASSING' signs every ten feet, this made an exclusive hunting ground for the Davidson's. We would park on the old Duthie Hill Road and hike over the hill. We had just returned to my 1967 Ford three-quarter-ton pickup and were driving up the road when we saw this guy walking up the road. He looked like his mother had dressed him and sent him out to play in a blizzard. He had so much clothing on that his arms just stuck out to the side and he had a rifle strapped to his back.

I told Larry, "Look, the Pillsbury boy has gone huntin'." The deer didn't need to worry, a buck could have fathered a set of twins and grew two more points on the rack before Pillsbury could have fired a shot.

I stopped and ask if we could give him a lift, and he said, "That would be great, I'm parked two miles up the road." I told him to hop in the back. When I thought that he had time to get in I took off. Larry hollered, "Oh shit, he ain't in!" I looked in the mirror and seen him hanging on the end gate with one foot up on the bumper and the other one stepping along like he was riding a scooter. I hit the brakes and then heard a hell of a crashing noise when he rolled up and hit the cab. Larry said, "Oh shit, well I guess he's in now," so I took off again.

Larry hollered, "Stop! Stop! Shit, he's falling out the back." I looked in the mirror and he was hanging over the end gate with his ass in the air and his legs pumping to beat hell. Again, I hit the brakes and that was followed by another loud thud against the cab and Larry saying, "He's in again."

I said, "What the hell is with him? Can't he hang on? He's like hauling a damn cow with roller skates on."

We stopped at the top of the hill and were letting him out, and I thought I had heard him say thanks so I took off. Larry hollered, "Hold it. Oh shit, he landed on his head, oh ouch. Yep I bet that hurt. He's getting up. Better keep going though, he's shaking his fist." Then Larry said, "Dale, what the hell did you take off for?"

I answered, "When I heard him say thanks I thought he was clear of the truck."

Larry said, "He didn't say thanks, he said 'THANK GOD.'"

"Well, what's he thanking God for? I'm the one that give him a ride."

Larry rolled his eyes upward and said, "Yeah, I'm sure that he really appreciated it."

HIC

IC

Miller 2005

Ma's Ducks

Also about this time (early sixties), Dad decided to dig a pond to drain the swamp. He hired a dragline (a big bucket on a crane) and started digging over one of the larger springs that bubbled water to the surface year round. When finished we had a small lake about a quarter of an acre in size and more than ten feet deep in the middle, and we soon filled it with 1,000 rainbow trout. There is a little stream that runs off the over flow and finds its way to the Snoqualmie River. We mowed lawn all the way around the pond and we built a cookout with a cedar shake roof with a four-foot wide barbecue. On holidays when all the kids were home we would have a picnic and the kids would swim and run races around the pond.

One year Mom said, "I want two pair of mallard ducks

for the pond. Dale, you and Joe find me some." It was soon decided that the best place to get a few ducks would be Lake Sammamish. The people living on the lake and the visitors at the park fed them so much that they could barely fly, so we figured that with salmon dip nets and the speedboat we could pick a few right out of the air.

We put the boat in at the public ramp and Joe idled the boat out to a flock of a few hundred. With Wayne on the port side and myself on the starboard, our nets ready, Joe hit the throttle and we were off. We each netted a duck about the same time but found that at thirty-five miles per hour a duck will go through the webbing and not even slow down. Damn, we needed two new salmon nets and a better plan.

I remembered that the parking lot for the Penny's store in Kirkland was right on Lake Washington and there were always ducks there, so I drove down there with a bag of popcorn. I parked in the shade, tied a piece of twine to the passenger door, shoved the door open and sat behind the steering wheel. I threw the popped corn out on the ground and soon had several ducks feeding. I spilled some on the floor and two pair of mallards hopped in the pickup. I pulled the door shut and left for home. By the time I got home the inside of the truck had popped corn, feathers and duck shit everywhere, but I had Ma's ducks. I pulled in by the pond and opened the door and the ducks jumped right in. They were swimming around when Mom got there. Soon she was sitting in a lawn chair feeding them bread. And, for a while at least, all was good with the world.

Come spring Mom said, "I hope they nest and we can have little ones." Well that happened all right, over and over again, and soon we had more damn ducks than you could count. If Ma did try to feed them it wouldn't be from a lawn chair. She would be running and dodging and throwing bread over her shoulder with a hundred ducks chasing her. It was about this time that she said, "Dale get rid of them damn ducks and don't be thinking of shooting them! I want you boys to catch them all. I'll go get on the phone and find them a new home."

Well, I didn't think that I could fit a hundred ducks in the front of my pickup, but brother Joe's truck had a canopy on the back. And if we could catch them, it would hold them okay—but we still had to catch them.

We had an old gillnet in the barn and it would reach across the pond. The plan was to wait until night with brothers on both sides of the pond to walk it along and catch ducks. It didn't work all that well, and we still had to catch about eighty more.

They really liked bread and we would get a few of them by throwing the net over them but they soon caught on to this plan were too fast for us. We had to slow them down a little so a new plan was hatched: let's get the bugger's drunk!

We mixed a fifth of gin and a fifth of whiskey in a pan and got two loaves of bread, soaked them in the booze and started feeding the ducks on the lawn. It wasn't long and we had them all. Joe had to rescue one, old Drake, that had staggered into the pond and was swimming around with his head under the water.

We reported to Ma that we had all of them in the back of the pickup and she said, "Good. The farmerette up on Stillwater Hill wants them all, and she is waiting for you to bring them." (Some people said the farmerette was a retired prostitute—others said, "She ain't retired.") When we got there, we backed up to the pond and started setting the ducks out on the ground. I looked over at the woman and she looked a little startled and asked, "Are they all right? They're acting a little peculiar."

I replied, "They will be okay in no time, they're just a little car sick from the ride up. You know like motion sickness." She nodded yes, and we said we had to get going and took off. In a day or so she called Mom and said all of the ducks were doing fine. The motion sickness lasted for the remainder of the first day and the quacking wasn't ducklike at all. She said that some of them just laid on their backs and watched their feet moving, others would walk around with their necks stretched out and heads sliding on the ground and staggering just like they were drunk.

Speeder Hunting

One evening Dad, my brothers and I were sitting around on the patio behind the house when we heard a speeder coming up the tracks. It was late for a motorcar and we all looked to Dad for the answer. He said that it was probably old Ted (the section foreman) and Roy (assistant foreman) going poaching for deer. When they went by we could see a case of beer and a rifle so we knew that Dad was right, they were motoring up the tracks to do a little hunting. In the workshop Dad had his electrical repair equipment and supplies and he had a headlight for a locomotive. (My Grandpa Gil's brother, Ernie, worked for Great Northern Railroad in the Everett yard, and I think that it came from there.)

The candlepower of that lamp was tremendous.

Someone suggested that we ought to rig up the old locomotive light and scare the hell out of them when they
came back down the tracks. Dad said that it would be easy
to power it and we could use the orchard ladder set up on
the tracks and it would be about the right height. We had a
couple hours to set up and test, and we had it perfected
enough to fool a pair of old railroad guys that had been
drinking.

It was good and dark when we heard them coming down
the grade and across the trestle over Griffin Creek. We
turned on the light and when they rounded the curve we
could see the sparks flying from all four wheels as old Ted
locked up the brakes. They jumped off the car, grabbed the
handles and lifted the car off the tracks just as we turned off
the light. We heard Ted say, "Hell yes, it was a goddamn

train, but where the hell did it go?" In the dark we ran out and got the ladder and light and were listening to Ted tell Roy, "I have seen a hell of a lot of trains in my life and that was a damn train, sure enough." They got the speeder back on the tracks and went by real slow and we could see that they had a deer.

A few years later dad had repaired an electric motor for Ted and he was at the shop to pick it up. He looked up in the corner and stopped dead in his tracks when he sawn the headlight. Dad said that you could see the light in his brain come on and Ted said, "Is that a light for a locomotive?" Dad said, "Well, yes, Ted, that is exactly what it is."

Ted followed with, "Damn you, Vern! I almost quit drinking over that little episode."

The No-Insurance Salesman

All the Davidson brothers worked at the mill when needed, such as when there was a big order that was too much for three of us to handle. Our cousin Gary was raised with us and he was as close as any brother so he brought the number to six. We pretty much dressed the same and all wore old Stetson hats that we converted from western wear to stylish sawmill. The hat had to be soaked until it was good and wet, then a deflated soccer ball would be inserted inside and blown up to the appropriate head size. The hat would then be left by the old stove in the mill office until it dried. It would keep its shape and keep the sawdust from going down the neck of one's hickory shirt.

One time a guy stopped for gas at Tolt with a truck of lumber and the local fellow pumping the gas asked him, "Have you come from the mill at the Davidson's?"

The driver said, "Yes, I think that they are kind of a strange bunch. What's with the hats? Are they Mormon?"

The local laughed and said, "No, I know them damn brothers real well and I can assure you that there ain't a Mormon in the bunch."

Speaking of assuring, about this time we had an insurance salesman that would come by and for little of nothin', he'd write us all policies that soon proved to be worth just that—"nuthin t'all." We called him the "no-insurance" salesman.

We would sit around the old stove in the mill office and think up stories like, "You know that you have a no-insurance policy when your hunting dog gets hit by the train and killed while chasing chickens. You would be covered, and they would send to you, at no cost, an almost new garbage bag to bury him in. However, if you injured your back while digging the grave, you would be considered 'gravely' injured. And the policy only covers minor injuries, so you would be considered to be shit out of luck and your claim would be buried also."

And speaking of burying, Dick was working and staying at the mill about this time and one day showed up and said that Weyerhaeuser had laid off all the timber fallers and he needed to work for a few days. He was with us for about ten years. Anyway, the no-insurance salesman was determined to write Dick some insurance. Dick was telling him, "I have no car, no house, no kids and I don't think I'm still married, but if a ever get to Sultan and see Marie that's the first thing that I'm going to ask her."

The no-insurance salesman wouldn't give up and said, "How about burial insurance? Do you have that?"

"I got better," says Dick, "I've got burial assurance."

The salesman said, "You mean insurance."

Dick said, "No, I mean assurance. That's when I'm dead and start to stink, I am assured that the boys here will bury me. You just can't go wrong with good assurance."

Joie — It's as Long as It's Tall

Joie was another of our guys at the mill. One day, in the pouring rain, old Joie had a ten-foot 2 x 6 standing on end and trying to measure it from the top down. He'd get down close to the ground with the measuring tape and the board would fall over and he would start all over again.

I opened the window and hollered at him, "Lay the damn board on the chain and measure it."

He turned and yelled back, "I don't give a damn how long it is—I have to have one ten feet tall."

I yelled back, "Joie! It's as long as it's tall," and closed the window.

After he got the ten-footers loaded he came in the office chuckling and saying, "It's as long as it's tall...that's a good one Dale, but you don't understand. I'm a building a shed to park my tractor and with me sitting on the seat I figure I need it to be ten feet tall and so I really didn't give a damn how long they are."

I looked at the serious look on his face and said, "Well, thank you Joie, for clearing that up for me."

He said, "Hell, that's okay Dale. You didn't know what I was going to build."

I told brother Joe once that old Joie was one of a kind and when they made him the must have threw away the mold. Joe said, "What makes you think they even used one?"

Joie and the Layin' Hens

I had some laying hens and they were in a molt and quit laying. When this happens they really start putting on weight and looking good, but no eggs. I saw Joie parked by the pen and looking at the dozen hens and soon here he came into the mill office and said, "Sell me those chickens."

I thought this out and said, "Joie, they are yours but I'd have to have twenty dollars for them."

He said, "Sold! I'll go and build some nest in my shed," and off he went.

Wayne said, "Hell Dale, you ain't going to charge him twenty bucks for laying hens that don't lay, are you?"

"Yep, I am," I said, "If I were to just give them to him he would get suspicious and not take the hens and I want to get rid of them."

Wayne said, "Dale, you ain't thinking this out. Hell, when there ain't no eggs old Joie will know that he'd been had and just bring them back."

I said, "Wayne, you can buy a hell of a lot of eggs for twenty bucks."

He started to grin and said, "Oh shit, this is going to be a good one," and it was.

We would go down into the alley behind old Joie's and load the nests up and go back to the mill and wait for the morning egg production report and Joie would soon show up tell us the difference between home-grown and store-bought eggs was remarkable. By the time the twenty bucks was gone (about thirty dozen) the hens had started laying on their own but nothing like when we were helping out. Joie blamed this drop in production on the feed and he said the world was going to "hell in a hand basket" and that you couldn't even buy good laying mash anymore.

You Can Grow Anything You Want with Horse Shit

Joie would come into the mill and he wouldn't say "Hi," "Kiss my ass," or anything like a greeting. He would just start talking, like he did this one time. He came busting in the door and announced, "Dale, you can grow anything you want with horse shit."

I said, "Oh yeah? How's that Joie?"

He told me, "Back in Illinois we had forty acres that my dad covered with twelve inches of horse shit then planted it with spuds. Every family in Chicago was eating our spuds."

I said, "Joie, a foot thick on forty acres is a lot of horse shit."

He said, "You're damn right it is and we only had but

two horses at the time." He left with a laugh and you always wondered what the hell he'd have to say next.

UNC

I don't think I could write a book and not mention Unc, a close family friend. His nickname was Uncle and over the years it just got shortened to Unc. All the stories about him involve his very poor eyesight. For several years my brother Joe, Joie and Unc all worked for the King County road department out of the Fall City division. Unc and Joie both lived in Tolt (Carnation) and for a short time shared a ride to work. Fall City is six miles south of Carnation. Joie told the story that Unc would park in front of the neighbor's house two doors away at 6:30 in the morning and honk. When Joie walked over and got in, Unc would ask, "What the hell you doing over at the neighbors when you knew I'd be here to pick you up?"

Joie said, "I just started driving my own self. I couldn't have him honking all over the damn neighborhood at 6:30 in the damn morning. My neighbors aren't that fond of me anyway and sometimes he's clear over on Bird Street, the next street over."

Unc was fond of duck hunting and he was hunting along the Snoqualmie River by Duvall when a farmer nicknamed Pinky was waist deep in a ditch and digging with a long-handled shovel. Unc crawled up and shot him with a good dose of #6 birdshot. Pinky let out a yell and Unc, realizing that he made a mistake, ran to help his good friend out of the ditch. Pinky said, "Unc what the hell did you shoot me for?" Unc's reply was, "With your white tee-shirt and the handle you looked just like a snow goose taking off." Years later we were all in the Cedar Log Tavern in Tolt and somebody said, "Hey Unc, tell us about the time you shot the snow goose." Unc turned and said, "I didn't shoot a snow goose and don't be telling that! Hell! They're on the endangered species list."

I broke in with, "And Pinky ain't on the list."

Unc laughed and said, "Now you got it right!"

One summer afternoon we were in the Cedar Log and Unc pulled out his pocket watch (he couldn't see well enough to see the dial) and he said, "Dale what time is it?" I told him it was ten minutes to two and he says, "Is that your pickup in front? I need to go home and put a roast in the oven (two block away). I've been drinking all day and I don't think I could walk that far."

I told him, "Unc, that's Joe's truck but we will take you." I told Joe that Unc had to run home and off we went. In the livingroom they had two television sets. One was set up in the corner with a straight back chair right in front of it. Unc said that from across the room it was just a white light to him and he had to put his nose on the screen to see what they were doing inside. When we got there, Unc got a big beef roast out of the freezer and said, "It will just take me a minute to flour and brown this and put it in the oven." Joe and I were sitting just outside the door in lawn chairs drinking a beer when old Unc started cussing. Here he came chasing his dog out the door saying, "That thieving son of a bitch stole the roast." We all went in the kitchen and helped look but we couldn't find it anywhere. Unc said, "Well, there's nothing to do but start over again."

He went to the freezer and got a huge roast and said, "Let's see the bastard try and pack this one off." He opened the flour bin and said, "I'll be damned!" There was the first roast. Unc said, "Well, one thing's for sure…"

I said, "Oh what's that Unc?"

"You and Joe are coming to dinner," he replied, "otherwise my wife is going to wonder why I cooked a whole hind quarter of a beef."

While we were driving back to the tavern I asked Unc, "Don't you feel bad about putting the blame on your poor old hunting dog?" His reply was "Hell No! That bastard will sit right there and look you in the eye and lie about everything else, why wouldn't he lie about the roast? Besides, he would have stole it in a minute if I hadn't hid it from him. Damn dog, anyway. And now I got forty pounds of roast in the oven. Hey, if you guys see anybody at the tavern that we know, invite them to dinner, okay? I don't recognize anybody unless they talk to me, and we need to invite more people to dinner."

Big Limb

In a corner of the barn we put in a walk-in cooler and a complete cutting and wrapping room. I would cut up deer, beef and pork. The cooler could hang three beef and a couple of deer at the same time. Our family would consume five beef a year. In the sixties, one brother, one sister and I had started our own families and Dad raised beef on the home place for all of us. Over the years I have learned that there are two ways to cut up a beef. The family way, when you know the size of the family and you cut and wrap accordingly, and the other way, which is the high-dollar way and you cut to get the most expensive cuts. I prefer the family way. My Mother can double wrap and keep up with me cutting. She is short and my brothers and I are all tall and she doesn't get in the way at all. We just pass everything over her head. A close family friend showed me a great deal, especially butchering hogs, and I always enjoyed cutting with Tom. We were cutting one time and a person come up in the conversation whose mental state might be of question and Tom said, "Big limb."

I replied with, "Big limb? Do you mean like, he doesn't have a full string of fish?"

"Yeah, that's the same thing," and he told me this story.

Back in West Virginia there was this large family with several married daughters and a neighbor girl (not married) who had a son that wasn't quite right from birth. The neighbor girl had a problem accepting this, and she was always making excuses for Tommy. One day the married daughters, the neighbor girl and the old mother were all sitting on the front porch rocking in the swings with Grandma in her rocker smoking her pipe and all the kids playing in the yard. One spoke up and said, "Tommy is sure getting big." Another sister said, "Nice looking, too."

Tommy's mother sighed and said, "Yes, but you know he just ain't been right ever since that big old limb fell out of the tree and hit him on top of the head." The sisters all sighed and said, "Yes, that's right."

Grandma didn't say anything, just kept rocking and smoking. They all looked at her and she finally spoke and said, "Well that must have been a hell of a limb 'cause it 'tetched' the whole damn family."

Every now and again Debra (the last wife) and I might see someone that we think might be acting a little strange and I'll say, "Big limb," and if she agrees she will say, " Big old limb."

Brotherly Love — NOT!

In Duvall there were two men married to sisters and the brothers-in-law had no brotherly love for one another at all. In fact, they hated each other. And they were always in some kind of a family financial disagreement over the wives' inheritances. Red was a very down-to-earth, hard-working, heavy-drinking guy that was well liked and rarely wore a suit. Bob wasn't very well liked and never wore anything but a suit.

On this one particular day a big argument started in the bank and soon spilled out into the street and Red called Bob a "no-good, thieving, yellow-bellied son of a bitch," and everyone there cheered.

Bob pointed at Red and said, "I am going to sue you for slander," and he turned and went into the local law office. Sure enough, shortly thereafter, it came out in the paper that the case would be tried in the courthouse in North Bend. I worked right across the street from there at the telephone office, so I got there early and got a good seat.

The courthouse filled up and some were standing out on the street. The old judge started with, "On such and such a date it states here Red, that you called Bob a 'no-good, thieving, yellow-bellied son of a bitch.' Does that sound about right to you?"

"Damn right, Judge," said Red, "that is exactly what he is."

"No," said the judge, "I mean, did you call Bob them names?"

"Hell yes, I did, and I'll do it again right now if you want."

"No, Red, that won't be necessary," said the Judge. "But by your own admission, this court finds you guilty and fines you fifty dollars. Pay the clerk at the door."

Red said, "Now let me get this straight. It cost fifty bucks to call Bob a son of a bitch?"

The judge said, "That's right. Pay on your way out."

Red stated, "If that's all it costs, I'll just pay for another one. I'm already in court." He turned to Bob and said, "Bob you are still a no-good, thieving, yellow-bellied son of a bitch! Thanks Judge, I'll leave an extra fifty at the door."

Went to Collection

A new BMW drove in to the mill one day and a wealthy lady from Bellevue was looking for a small bag of red cedar sawdust for her wardrobe closet. She said that it made all of her clothes smell heavenly. No problem, we were cutting more than 10,000 feet a day and wallowing in red cedar sawdust. I asked her how I smelled to her and she didn't say anything. I guess the sweat was overpowering the heavenly smell, but she did tell her husband, "Oh look, they are making brand new old barn boards."

We did saw a lot of barn boards. We cut the lumber for the biggest barn to be built in Snohomish County, and the very wealthy farmer decided that he paid us plenty and subtracted $2,000 from his check when he mailed it to us with a note saying that he wouldn't be paying the rest. I decided that I would drive down and pay him a little visit and introduce him to our collection specialist, Mr. Winchester. I got out of the pickup and started poking shells into the rifle when he come running out and said, "Dale, what the hell are you going to do with the gun?" I told him that when I get really pissed off I usually felt better after I shot something and I thought that maybe he had too damn many cows anyway.

He said, "Dale, please don't shoot nothing and I'll be right back with your money. Would cash be okay?"

I said, "Yes, but you had better add a hundred beings it went to collection."

He said, "Fair enough."

When I got back to the mill and told Wayne that we got paid in full and how it happened he said, "What if he didn't pay, Dale? Would you have shot some cows?"

I said "Yeah, eight."

He asked, "Why eight?" And I showed him that I only had eight bullets with me.

The Swiss Matador

Big Al had the dairy farm across the highway from the Big Rock Road in Duvall. He was a close friend and also a good customer for sawdust and special cut lumber and timbers. He was always building or remodeling barns, loafing sheds, silage pits and corrals, so I would see him on a weekly basis.

Also, both Al and I had sons on the high school basketball team and we would attend all the games. Big Al was one of the strongest men I ever saw. He was just six feet tall and 265 pounds of solid muscle. When he was in his late twenties and early thirties he held the world championship in Swiss wrestling. He told me that this was a contest like the Japanese sumo and then laughed and said the only difference was instead of that towel pulled up your ass, the Swiss wore a nice leather skirt. Al also wrestled professionally under the name Sailor. I could always spot Al at a good distance, not only because of his size but he wore the same type of clothes every day. Tank top, or shirt with the sleeves

115

ripped off at the shoulder (because his arms were massive), bib overalls and the ever-present sailor cap.

We had gas, diesel and oil products delivered to the mill and every now and then Al would have us get him a fifty-five gallon barrel of motor oil. He was driving his wife's Cadillac this time he stopped in to visit and I told him that a barrel of oil was there for him and the next time that I went to the farm I would bring it. He said, "I was hoping it would be here. I'll just put it in the trunk of the caddy." He popped open the trunk.

I said, "I'll get the forklift and strap."

His reply was, "Oh no! I've seen you run that damn thing and you'll scratch mama's car. I'd better load it myself." He walked over to the barrel, tilted it so that he could grab the bottom with one hand and he lifted it to his chest and gently set it in the trunk. When he drove out of the mill yard, the back bumper was almost touching the ground. I would guess that the barrel must have been between 450 and 500 pounds.

Al had raised a Holstein bull from a calf and when the thing was four years old it weighed over a ton. That bull could break his way out of every stall that was on the place, so Al ordered full dimension 2 x 12 to build a new stall, sixteen by sixteen feet, eight boards high. When Wayne and I had the log deck loaded with good sixteen-foot Douglas fir and were ready to start sawing I said, "Hell, lets make 3 x 12." So we did.

Several weeks after the new bull pen was done Al drove into the mill yard, and when he got out of his pickup I could see that he was bruised all over and his biceps were bluish yellow. I asked him, "What the hell got a hold of you?" He said that he was wrestling his little bull in the new pen and that it ended up a split decision. After he took a chair in the office I gave him a cup of coffee and said, "Al, what the hell were you doing getting in the stall with the bull?"

He told us that the bull had got cut up when he would break down the old stalls and he wasn't healing up, so the vet wanted to give him a shot and stitch up a cut on his underside. The two of them had got the bull to stick its head into the stanchion with grain and closed the latch. Then Al and the vet both entered the stall and the vet jabbed him with the needle. The bull let out a bellow and turned his head sideways and a horn popped through the bar. Another twist of his massive head and he was turned facing them. Al said that he was looking at them like, "Okay, who's got the needle?"

The vet took advantage of the pause and jumped behind Al and up the eight-foot wall into the rafters of the barn. When the crew built the stall and bolted the sideboards on, they left a three-inch space between the fourth and fifth board so you could look in from the outside. Not even thinking that the toe hold would come in damn handy if you were trying to climb the wall and get away from a bull that you had just jabbed in the ass with a big old needle.

Al said the next thing he knew he was in a 16 x 16 ring, circling eye to eye with an opponent that had a big weight advantage. The bull charged and Al, not knowing what else to do, side stepped and tried to get him in a headlock. The neck was so huge that Al said he had to settle for hooking his arm around the horns and get in close so that the bull couldn't drive him into the wall. Around and around they went doing the hokey pokey.

I said, "Wait a minute Al. Where the hell was the vet? Couldn't he distract the bull?"

Al said, "Hell no! He had the best seat in the house. He was just sitting up there wishing he had some popcorn to munch on while he was watching this match, man against beast."

Wayne piped in with, "Well, you're sitting here now, so how did you get out of there?"

Al continued and said that he realized that he had to think of something fast 'cause he was being thrown around like a rag doll. And, he was mad as hell that he had raised this son of a bitch and it was trying to kill him. They had just slammed into the wall again and the bull opened his mouth and bellowed. Al said, "I figured that the bull was going to get me and I just wanted to put a little hurt on him too so I shoved my arm down his throat and got his tongue in my fingers. I closed my hand around the soft flesh and began twisting and pulling with all my might. I felt the bugger shudder and I knew it must be hurting so I gave him another twist and he just stood there with his tongue out about a yard like he was in a trance, like a horse when you put a lip twitch on them.

"Boys I never seen anything like it, I would have liked to give him some more but I figured a tied match might be okay and I turned and went up the wall.

"I was just going over when he hit me in the ass and I fell into the stall on the other side and lost my wind when I hit the ground. The bull was trying to bust down the wall by standing on its hind legs and bringing the weight of his head and shoulder on the top board. But Dale, the 3 x 12 held; he couldn't break them down. Changing that order to three inch might have saved my life. At least it kept us from having a second round."

There was never a rematch and the bull went to the

butcher. Al said even the hamburger was tough, but he enjoyed every bite. A short time after that Al got a "new bull"—he drove a car and wore a rubber glove (artificial insemination).

Buster

My cousin Gary and I loved to hunt, and bird hunting was one of our favorite pastimes. Over the years I have raised hundreds of pheasants, cuckers (fowl that are a bit bigger than quail) and quail to be turned loose on the home place and this helped to train dogs. I had two golden labs from Carnation Farms—Carnation Burnt Sienna and Gunner 2— and they both turned out to be excellent dogs. I liked the labs because they were good with kids and would hunt water or land.

Gary had a German shorthair; it would point and that is about all it was good for. It was about as smart as a bag of hammers. He would point at anything from a mouse to a moose and he didn't seem to notice the difference. If a hunter in the next field over bagged a bird, old Buster would go right over there and bring us the bird, unless he was a little hungry. If that were the case then he would just eat it, feathers and all.

We liked to hunt ringneck pheasants in eastern Washington, and I would drive my pickup and camper with our jeep in tow. We would put the dogs in the backseat of the jeep and drive the canal roads out to the fields. Buster would never stay in the back and he would jump into the front when you wouldn't be expecting it and sometimes cause you to run off the road. The canals are cement and thirty feet wide, twelve to fifteen feet deep—you wouldn't want to run into one.

One time I was driving along and Buster saw a tweety bird, or some damn thing, and jumped over the seats. With his ass on the gas pedal and his body through the steering wheel, he was barking out the open window on my side of the jeep. We were going forty miles an hour along the canal with a sharp left hand turn coming up. I couldn't steer and that's when Gary turned off the ignition. We finally got to a farmer's house and he said that it would be okay if we parked there and hunted his property. We let the dogs out and he said, "That shorthair is the finest dog I have ever seen." Buster went over to a pen full of laying hens and went on point. Gary went over and kicked him in the ass and chased him away from the pen. We were almost in the

field when we realized that Buster was back on point at the chicken pen again. Gary ran back and Buster stayed on point long enough to get another good kick in the ass. He broke point and ran around to the other side of the pen.

He must have figured that we couldn't see a pen full of chickens, so he went up over the fence and ate one, then came back over the top with one in his mouth for Gary, which he handed over like the good bird dog that he was. Gary handed it, rather sheepishly, to the farmer. The farmer looked the bird over and said, "Look at that. This bird isn't hurt at all," as he tossed it over the fence into the pen. Then he exclaimed, "That's the finest dog I ever seen."

I couldn't believe what I was hearing and said, "What about the one he ate?"

He shrugged his shoulders and said, "He was probably just a little hungry."

I said, "I'll pay for the chicken."

The farmer laughed and slapped his leg and asked, "Why? You didn't get any of it. Now get out there and hunt. I want to watch that dog work." Buster hunted the best he ever did and when we returned to the farm I wanted to give the farmer a couple birds, which he took and thanked us and said, "If you ever want to get rid of that dog I want it. Damn that is a hell of a dog!"

"Yeah, it's a hell of an excuse for a dog," I said under my breath. A few months later Gary called and said that he was getting a divorce and he had to find a place for Buster to stay for a few days while he made a trip up north driving truck for Lynden transfer. When he got back he was going to go to eastern Washington and give Buster to the farmer. I said to bring him out and I would keep him until he got back from the run up north.

When Gary and Buster showed up, I went out to meet them and noticed Buster was limping and had some hide wore off his ass. I asked Gary what happened. Gary said, "You know he can't ride in the cab, so I fastened a short chain to the bed of the pickup. I was going through downtown Issaquah when a boxer said something to old Buster and he jumped out." Gary went on to tell that by the time he got over to the curb, old Buster was hanging there lifeless and had lost a patch of hide off his ass. Gary said, "I panicked and unsnapped the chain. The son of a bitch was faking and he took off down the street and beat the shit out of the boxer. The owner called the cops and said that I pulled over and sicked my dog on his dog." Others who witnessed came to Gary's defense and it was dismissed.

The week with Buster was long. I swear he would bark at himself if he couldn't find something else, and he barked all night long. When you fed him he would gulp it down so fast that he would usually barf it back up and eat it again. I decided that I would cure him of that and I made him a sandwich with a jar of that extra hot horseradish. I tossed it to him and he ate it in a gulp, then he went for the water dish and lapped it dry. I unsnapped the chain and he took off for the pond and dove right in and started drinking and swimming. It was amazing for a dog that didn't even like to get his feet wet.

When he finally came out on the lawn he scooted around pulling with his front legs with the hind legs sticking out and scooting his ass on the cool, wet grass. I fed him a can of dog food and he just looked at it. After a while he did eat, but he wasn't in any hurry. I went in the house and later the wife said, "What did you do to Buster? I haven't heard him bark once tonight."

Gary came the next day to take Buster to his new home

and he came in and said that he thought Buster's collar might be too tight. I asked, "Why do you think that?"

He replied, "When I drove in he was barking but no noise was coming out. He was like a damn mime or something. How long has he been pretending to bark?" I lied of course and said that I hadn't even noticed.

A couple of years later we were driving through Othello and there was Buster on the top of a pickup just laying there waiting for the farmer to come out of the store and go for home. We accepted the offer to go to the farm for a spell, and we sure got a kick out of the farmer and the best damn dog ever. Buster rode on the tractor for hours while the fields were being worked to be planted with field corn and sugar beets. The farmer stated that Buster was the most laid-back dog he had ever seen and he didn't really bark at all. I said, "So he doesn't bark much?"

"Nope, not a bit. Mostly he just pretends."

Driving home over Snoqualmie Pass I told Gary about Buster's favorite sandwich, you know, the one that he doesn't want to bark about. We were sure that the horseradish couldn't cause permanent damage; the only reasoning we could come up with was the hot radish burned his throat and barking must have irritated it, so he decided to give up barking out loud.

Fishing by Rail

When the export of logs to Asia reached its peak, most of the mills in the state shut down and never opened again. A load of #1 saw logs, about 4,500 board feet (Scribner scale), that used to cost about $450 was now $4,000. Lumber was still at $285 per/1,000 board feet. We keep the mill open by custom sawing and charging $75/1,000 board feet. Hauling would be paid by the customer.

Gary was driving for Lynden Transfer trucking company and making a six-day run to Alaska. He was hauling hanging beef in the first trailer and booze in the second trailer. The return trip he was bringing down frozen halibut and canned salmon. Sometimes he would call and tell me to pick him up at the big terminal in Seattle, not far from the King Street Railroad Station. I picked him up one time and he said, "Open the doors on the refrigerated trailer and grab yourself a halibut." When I looked in, the fish were stacked tight to the top. And when I pulled one (about seventy-five pounds) out of the center, half the load came out onto the dock. Gary said, "Don't worry about it. They have to unload them anyway," and we took off.

He didn't have to be back for four days and I would usually plan a fishing trip. The railroad was running a round-trip Casey Jones excursion trip (a ride on an old, restored train) from the King Street Station to eastern Washington and back on the same day. The old steam engine and passenger cars would be passing through the Howard Hanson Watershed at a slow enough speed that a pair of fishermen carrying a case of beer and fishing poles could just step off. We got a lot of smiles and looks when we handed the conductor our round-trip tickets, but we were soon under way.

When we got to the middle of the reservoir, I swear the train damn near stopped and the conductor waved goodbye and said, "See you in about four hours." Fishing was even better than I thought it would be and we were choosy with our limit. A watershed patrol pickup stopped and someone hollered, "Get the hell out of there. It's closed to fishing." We just kept on choosing keepers and here he came, walking out the railroad tracks to us. I had a copy of the Washington State fish and game laws and I showed him that Howard Hanson wasn't listed under "Closed to fishing." He agreed but said that it was closed to trespassing. I asked him who owned the railroad tracks? He said, "Hell, the railroad owned the damn tracks and that any dummy ought to know that."

I answered with, "That's what I thought. The train brought us here and will soon be picking us up," and I showed him my ticket stub and told him if he didn't have a ticket that he was the one trespassing. He left and said that he was calling the sheriff.

The train came and we were soon on board and showing the passengers our catch. The conductor came with a worried look on his face and said that there was a large gathering waiting for us at the station. The engineer had told him the sheriff and news media were set up on the landing dock. I said, "Damn, I'm sorry that we are going to miss that but our truck is parked at the trucking terminal about six blocks this side of the station. We'll be getting off

Cousin Gary Le Moine and a catch of rainbows from Howard Hanson Lake.

there." He gave us a big smile and said, "I'll tell the engineer to slow down for you."

Out Behind Camp

During the daily coming and going of the many bums past our house, sometimes it would be the same one staggering back and forth. If you watched awhile you would see that a lot of times they'd fall down, get back up and go in the opposite direction. I had one fellow ask me one time, "Did you see me walk here?" I responded that I hadn't. He said, "I don't know if I was coming from town or if I was going."

I asked him if he had money and he reached in his pocket and pulled out some wadded up bills and said, "Yes, I do have some." I told him that if he did have money that he must be going to town, and he said, "You are right!" He thanked me and said, "I best be going then."

I remember thinking how can it get so bad that you don't even know where you are or how you got there.

Now with the bum camp gone and the CYO Camp (Catholic Youth Organization) in its place, we just say out behind camp instead of out behind the bum camp. Out behind camp to a Davidson refers to the twenty-five or thirty square miles between Snoqualmie and Sultan with its maze of hundreds of miles of logging roads.

My brother Joe and I bought an old 1945 military Jeep with a metal cab and doors and a winch on the front. This purchase was made about 1962 and for the first ten years or so it was painted white as snow. Joe and I drank a little then and we would load a couple cases of beer in and go drive as many of the roads as we could on the amount of beer that we had with us. One time that I remember we were running low on beer and only had about two left when we come upon our neighbor's old station wagon parked on the side of the road. We looked and could see that he hadn't run off the road and that he could drive out of there okay. We figured that he must be fishing the beaver pond. We were just about to go when I saw that he had a full case of beer in the back of the wagon and that the car was unlocked. "What if we just took the beer and left some money?"

"Yeah, that would probably be okay. Do you have any money?"

"No."

"Damn, I don't either. Well hell, we can't steal a guy's beer. Wait! If he was stuck and we pulled him out he would give us the beer."

"Yes, he would. But he ain't stuck."

"No, but he could be." So with just a little nudge with the jeep it looked like he might be stuck. We then drove just around the corner out of sight, but within hearing range and opened our last beer. We didn't have to wait long and Joe said, "Do you hear that?"

I said, "Well, yes, it sounds like someone is stuck." We started on down there and he ran right out in front of the jeep and looked really pleased to see us. He said that he should have been more careful when he parked but he was excited to get to fishing. We pulled him out and said no to his trying to give us money. I told him, "That's what good neighbors are for."

He said, "How about a case of beer? I got one right here in the wagon."

I said, "Wow! Really? You got a case of beer in there?"

"Yep, Dale and it's yours, and I sure thank you guys."

Over the years we had heard people state that they only took a drink on special occasions and never before noon. Joe and I thought that this might be good discipline, so we made it a rule that we would not take a drink until we had seen at least one all white horse. You couldn't leave our home place at the time in any direction without seeing at least one. Every neighbor had a white horse. We could go to Sultan and play pool and drink all day and drive home because we didn't have to drive on a public highway. It was on the return from one of these serious drinking bouts that we loaded two cases of beer into the back of the jeep and were en route about twenty-five miles from anywhere with Joe driving.

Every now and again Joe and the road turned at the same time in the same direction. But we were not in any hurry and we were riding along just taking in the scenery when I noticed girls moving around in the woods on my side of the jeep. I didn't say anything to Joe and he seemed to be looking out his side of the jeep and just driving real slow when he just stopped and shut off the engine. We sat there a while drinking and he turned and asked, "Did you see anything unusual back there?"

And I said, "Nope. Why, did you?"

"Just some girls. But how can that be, way up here in the damn woods?"

"Well, now that you mention it I think I seen a couple too, and they looked like they were looking for something." We decided that we had better turn around.

There really were girls from the University of Washington. The school had moved several trailers and a

128

generator out in the gravel pit to house these students who were studying botany and collecting samples. They were gathering everything, including two guys that had a little to drink and more in the jeep. They were soon drinking beer and smiling at us and we were just smiling back when this old guy came along and said that it would be good if we left.

I said that I didn't think we were ready yet, and he said that he was calling the cops and left. The girls said to give them another beer and then we had better go before the cops got there. I told the fine ladies that there wasn't a phone within twenty-five miles and that he was bluffing. They said that he had a sheriff radio and he was probably on it already. We said good-bye.

About five miles down the road we met a 4 X 4 Bronco with the bubble gum machine on top with all lights flashing. He asked for directions and we sent him flying up the road to catch the bad guys. In haste, we must have taken a wrong turn somewhere, and we found ourselves looking at a sign that said Remlinger. We just couldn't believe that we were that close to home already. From Remlinger's Farm follow the river down to the bridge, take a left and go one mile and there will be home. It wasn't there. Our road was gone and the houses gone. I said to Joe, "Let me drive. Maybe you are doing something wrong." I couldn't find home either.

We went back to the Remlinger sign and a fellow that had been watching us came over and asked if he could help us find something. He said, "You appear lost." I told him that we were not lost but our house was gone. "Do you live around here?"

"Yeah, we used to, just down the river to the Tolt Bridge and to the left one mile."

He started laughing and called to his wife, "Come and look at these two drunks. They think that they're at Tolt." There was a Remlinger in Monroe at that time, too—eighteen miles away!

Flyin' Low

Out behind camp there are dozens of beaver ponds with trout in them, but it is so grown over with trees and brush you could look for one all day and not find a wet spot. Weyerhaeuser had very good maps and the ponds were all on there, but when you are riding in the jeep all of the side of the road look the same. I needed a better plan.

I had a friend in Fall City, also named Dale, and people said we had a lot in common. I didn't see it. Hell, he was crazy. People would say things like, "Do you know what that damn Dale did this time?" and the other one would say, "Which Dale?" And the first one would say, "Does it really even matter which one?"

Other Dale had a plane and he had been flying rather dangerously since he was about fourteen years old. I told him the plan and we loaded up with a five-gallon pail of old house paint, which I had mixed with water, and a tire pump and balloons. I cut the very end off the pump's hose and put it in the paint. When you pulled up, the handle to the cylinder would fill with the watered down paint and make it easy to fill several balloons. After locating a pond that we wanted to mark, the other Dale would take the airplane down and I would start throwing paint bombs and mark a straight path to the nearest road. I would hit the center of the road with a spot about four feet in diameter. It wouldn't last long, rain would soon wash it away, and if anyone came upon it they would probably think, "Damn, that had to be a big ol' seagull."

With the maps, paint bombs and a little crazy flying, it made locating beaver ponds rather easy.

Ma in the Hospital

In 2002 my eighty-five-year-old mother and my brother Joe were shopping in the Fred Meyer store in Monroe. Mom fell and hit her head and went to the emergency room at Monroe's Valley General Hospital. As soon as we got the call, my wife Debra and I caught the ferry off Lopez and charged down to see her.

I was put to ease as soon as she saw me and said, "Hell of a note. I have to fall on my head to get you off that damn island to come see me." That's my ma and I knew she was okay, although she was all bandaged up. She soon followed with, "Dale, you wouldn't believe how nice them people at Monroe Fred Meyer was to me."

"Oh? How's that, ma?"

"Well," she said, "they called the aid car and the nicest girl held a damp cloth to my head until the aid car got there."

My brother-in-law said, "They were probably afraid that they were going to get sued because it was in their parking lot."

"It wasn't their fault at all, and there won't be any talk as a lawsuit. They have very nice people over there and it's my own damn fault I fell down. I should have been looking where I was going," said Ma.

I bring this up only to help show how we were raised. You were responsible for your own problems and couldn't blame someone else. Mom is eighty-nine now and doing fine. When I left the hospital that day I asked Mom if she needed anything. She said, "No, but I'm tired and want to take a little nap. The railroad tracks are right out back and that damn train came flying through here at two a.m. and woke me and I couldn't go back to sleep."

Brother Joe piped up with, "Why couldn't you go back to sleep? Did the train make you horny?!"

"Joe!!! Don't talk like that in here. You don't know who might be listening. Dale, get him the hell out of here so I can take a nap." When I closed the door, she already had her eyes shut. I could only see one eye because of the bandage, but I could see a grin so I knew she must have seen the humor in Joe's one-liner. I thought it was one of his best ever.

Q-6i-cheeses

Every now and again I get to leave the island and go to see my mom. It's a forty-five minute ferry ride to Anacortes and 100 miles south to Carnation/Tolt. Most times as soon as she sees me it's, "I'll put the coffee on and after you say hi (to my brothers at the mill). You come sit with me and we will have a catch up on everything." I find that we both revisit the past in our dreams at night and sometimes she will start our visit with, "You won't guess who I dreamt about the other night. Not in a million years would you guess so I might as well tell ya."

"You're probably right, Mom, I don't have a clue. Who was it?"

"Do you remember old Herman Amslear? It was him and he looked just like when he was our neighbor, and I was a kid on the old Tolt farm."

His face was coming to me in my mind and I said, "Oh, by Jesus."

Mom laughed and said, "Yep, you remember him then. And, yes, he did say that a lot, didn't he?"

My Grandpa, Gil Boersma, and his team, Rock and Rye, Tolt Farm.

"Hell yes, Ma, the start and end of every sentence. Do you remember your dad [my Gramp Gilbert Boersma] telling about when he got that new work horse from up at Lynden?"

"Oh, by Jesus, yes." She laughed.

If you go north out of Carnation about a mile you will come to the Carnation Farm Road on your left. The Tolt farm was on that corner and the barns and house have been gone for about forty years I would guess. Amslear's place was across the road, the barn right on the road, which is still there now. The story Gramp told was that when the horse arrived, so did Herman, "Oh by Jesus, Gil, that horse is a looker. Oh, by Jesus, strong, too! Oh, by Jesus, you've got a fine horse there. Well, by Jesus, I'd better get home. By Jesus, yes, I'd better be going." And away he went.

I said, "Ma, I never felt like he was swearing though, even as often as he used that phrase."

Mom said, "Oh no, me neither. I think at one time it was something like 'Oh by the grace of Jesus it's a fine day,' and things like that. And he just shortened it up so he could get more of them in." Well, we get as many of these visits in as we can and I really feel like we visit these people of the past. And I am sure that there is a heaven where we will all be together again. And, oh, by Jesus, I hope that it's kind of a big old bum camp up yonder.

Bobo

Every now and again Debra and I will catch the ferry and

go over to America (the mainland) and do some shopping. It seems like most of the time we shop too long and really have to fly to catch the boat back home.

It was one of those days and we were heading west on spur twenty from Burlington to Anacortes. The railroad parallels the highway and, most of the time, I am the passenger, so I was just looking out the window and saw a work train and a small crew working on the tracks.

When there is a low spot in the track it can be fixed by a machine that is known as a Gandy Dancer. It lifts and tamps crushed rock and makes the tracks level again. When I was a kid, that job would have required a crew with as many as fifty men. By using big hand-operated jacks, they would raise the rail and tamp in crushed rock all by hand—sometimes this could mean twenty men to a rail. The crew would arrive in their own converted boxcars that they called home and may well have stayed in the area for as long as a year, so we would get to know some of them real well. One of the crew foremen was nicknamed Bobo, and he dated and married a local girl named Delores.

My mother has a good friend named Annie; they went to school together and have been close friends all these years (about eighty-seven). Annie, living closer to the gossip in town, still calls Mom and gives her the news. This one morning Annie called and told Mom that Bobo had just up and died for no reason. At this time there was another Bobo living at Woodland Park Zoo. He was a huge gorilla. Mom's answer to Annie, "What the hell? Did he get a peanut crosswise or something?" It was met with silence and the phone going dead. Mom didn't think much of it because the phone did go dead every now and again. After a couple days went

Debra (the last wife) and Dale on Lopez, 2005.   Photo: Ron Hall.

by and no updates from her friend mom thought that it was unusual and that she had better get her on the wire. Annie answered and Mom knew right off that something must be wrong, so she says, "Annie are you mad at me for something?"

Annie replied that she thought mom could have shown a little concern over Bobo's death. Mom said, "I would have but I didn't know that you were so damn fond of the monkey."

Well that got a reply from Annie all right, and she says, "Who in the hell you calling a monkey? You hardly knew him!"

Mom's reply was, "Knew who?"

Annie says, "Delores' husband!"

Well, it got straightened out okay and Mom felt bad. Her and Annie's friendship continues, and I enjoy hearing them tell their stories still today.

SO we were still driving along and I was thinking about this when I hear Debra saying, "Well, I can tell buy your smile that you are not listening to me."

I looked at my watch and told her that it was going to be real close on catching the ferry. She just started shaking her head and says, "What do think that I have been saying for the last five minutes? You went away again for a while didn't you? One of these days it's going to be straight to the old folks' home, and I think its right around the corner."

And I say, "I didn't know that there is one right close to here." More shaking of the head.

Words of Wisdom

Just the other day I asked my wife, "How long have we been married?"

She said, "I'll leave that up to you and your answer might determine how long we are going to stay married."

I said, "Hon, be serious. Is it fifteen or sixteen years now?"

I was being serious, so she answered, "Yes, it's been sixteen years. Good guess, dear. Why do you ask?"

"Just a little research for my book. Do you still love me?"

"Yes, Dale, most of the time anyway," she answered. Now if you find that this conversation is a little silly and childlike you are dead wrong. This is what is known to the smart man as a little marriage maintenance and a smart man will tell his wife every chance that he gets that he loves her.

Debra (the last wife).   Photo: Ron Hall

Also, he should tell all of his children every time he talks to them, no matter if his sons are six feet two inches or six feet four inches tall and 245 pounds (like mine). You tell every one of them that you love them. Especially tell your mom, even if she's eighty-nine years old and has heard it hundreds of times—it's important.

Every now and again when I really get into a story I might put the wrong name to the wife (even though there's only two). Debra will say, "No, Dale. Arlene will be your first wife. You were married to her for twenty-six and a half years. I'll be Debra, your last wife of sixteen years" (the research). Oh, by Jesus, did I say the wrong one again? Oh by Jesus, a guy wouldn't want to do that too often. Did you get the last wife part?

Speaking of last things, I wouldn't want to leave you with the idea that wine is bad. The poison that the bums drank was fortified. The alcohol was added, like gasoline to skim milk—nothing like the care and time that it takes to make real wine. "Dago red" was made with loving care and a knowledge that has been handed down for centuries. I do not and never have drunk wine. I went through a treatment center in 1975 for alcoholism and I choose not to drink today. But my wife, Debra (the last one), likes a glass of good wine with dinner and I enjoy looking and maybe finding a good wine that she might like.

Promise You'll Write a Book

It was at the treatment center when I was first told that I should write a book. In the last week or so of the program the time comes when you go meet with the shrink and he asks, "Why did you hate your mother?" Well our visit started with, "Dale it says here that you were raised right up the road in Carnation, is that correct?"

And I answered, "Yep, Doc, that's right."

"All right then, tell me all about your childhood and don't leave anything out."

I told him a few stories and I noticed that he wasn't writing anything down at all. I didn't know if this was a good sign or not but he did have a big grin and I felt okay with telling him more. I just finished with stabbing the old chicken farmer in the ass and that old neighbor lady telling everybody that I had a mean streak when he threw back in his chair, hands over his head, laughing so hard that he was having a hard time breathing. I got a little concerned and asked if I could get him something. When he could manage to speak and was trying to find the pencil that he had thrown over his head and into the corner, he said, "Yes, you can get the hell out of here before you cause me to have a heart attack or something."

"Are you sure, Doc? It's only 11:20 and we were set to go till noon."

He just pointed to the door and kept dabbing at his eyes with his hankie. I left there thinking that therapy was a good thing and it didn't take up all that much of your time.

If he would spot me in the lunchroom he would come join me and always ask for a quick bum story. A week or so after that I had completed my stay and my wife Arlene (the first one) had come to gather me up to go home. Doc walked me to the door and said, "Dale, you are going to be okay, but I want you to do something for me."

I said, "Sure, Doc, what is it?"

He said, "Promise me that you will write a book."

I told him, "No problem. Hell, I might even write more than one." The year then was 1975. (Old Herman would have said, "Oh, by Jesus, 'twas nineteen sebenty and five.")

Tʜₑ Bus Drⁱⱱₑr

One of the patients at the treatment center was a Greyhound bus driver. He had thirty-seven years driving bus without any traffic tickets or accidents. This was an amazing record considering that he drank a fifth of whiskey every day.

In our room at the center there were three beds, and when he came to us he was given the center bed. He slept for the first forty-eight hours. I woke up in the night hearing him talking on the phone. He was saying that they got him off the bus that he was driving to Spokane from Seattle at Ellensburg and they sent him to Monroe for treatment. I was just falling back to sleep when I realized, hell, we didn't have a phone in our room and I turned on the light. He was sitting on the edge of the bed and talking in his shoe. I grabbed the shoe and threw it into the closet and told him to go to sleep. I had just got to sleep again and I heard him talking away again, they must have called him on his other shoe because when I turned on the light there he was talking into his other shoe. I threw that shoe in the closet with the other one and told him that they didn't allow any calls after 10:00 p.m. He said that

Dale, Deb and Ana, our first grandchild,1987, now enrolled at Washington State to be a nurse.

nobody had bothered to tell him that and that the person that kept calling was a pain in the ass and it wasn't any of their damn business if he was in treatment. I told him, "Oh, by Jesus, you are right, let's get some sleep."

He didn't get any more calls that night, but I'll be damned if they didn't have the nerve to call him back on both shoes a few nights later. I learned that his wife had died of cancer and that his only son had returned from Vietnam in a wheelchair and died in an alley in Tacoma of an overdose. The only thing that he had left was his job and the bottle, and damned if that wasn't being taken away also. He said once that "these damn people who say, 'Don't drink and drive' had damn sure never drove a bus."

He said, "Dale do you know the type people that ride a Greyhound?"

I said that I didn't think that I did know any of them firsthand. He said, "If you did, you wouldn't even think of driving a damn bus sober." He added that people that say "Don't drink and drive" more than likely hadn't tried it, and if they did they would find that it made the trip go a lot easier.

When I left the center he was still there (thank God) and, damn, I didn't get the phone number to his shoe so I lost contact with him. I do every now and again think about the poor guy and that the only thing left in life that was important to him was drinking and driving. He drove that same route for years and would pay people to hide a bottle in the hand towel dispensers at every stop; one of these people finally made the call. The state patrol had to chase the bus down to get him out from behind the wheel.

In one of our private talks he told me that he regretted encouraging his son to join the service and I was a very lucky man to have my children in good health. I think that it is very easy for a man to tell his daughters that he loves them; I think that it should be just as easy to tell your sons, too. And I do it every time I talk to them and they tell me the same. The bus driver gave me this wisdom and I won't be forgetting it, ever.

One Last Thing

Moving right along, and still speaking of "last things" I want to leave you with, I want to believe that you might have found a little of the love and humor that I've put in these pages. I also hope that you haven't been offended with the limited vocabulary that I write with. I have already been told that it is not politically correct to use the word, "dwarf."

Well, I can't describe my little friend without using it, and that's the word that he used when he told me that his twin sister was a dwarf, too. He used the word, so I think he would be fine with me using it, too. Early in life as a small boy I could get past all of that and not let it keep me from knowing that great big heart in that little body. He couldn't drive me away with a screaming fit and I'm glad that, for the most part, I can see beyond that sort of stuff.

As a society, we are so correct that we let so-called misfits and winos lie in the street and die. We even give them a good name, like "homeless" after we close the home that they lived in. Damn it, people, am I the only person with the knowledge that if you don't interfere in that drunk or druggie's life that they will surely die? We did away with a system that worked because somebody said that it wouldn't be proper for us to tell people how to live. But why are we still telling people all over the world how they can live and ignoring our duty to those on our own streets? I know that I'm not alone in my thinking. Americans don't enjoy seeing the less fortunate die.

Right or wrong, the bum camp gave a lot of people a place to live and a little dignity. Almost everything at the camp was donated, such as beds and bedding from hospitals, drugs, as well as food and clothing. Would a camp work now in 2005? Yes—it would mean that others would have to get involved in the lives of the less fortunate, but it would work. The hard part would be replacing Prince, but I think we might find a good-trained German shepherd that would be ready to retire from the force to take charge and run a good camp. Then, oh, by Jesus, it would be rather easy, I would think, to just let the people live their way out of the problem with a little help.

I was thinking about things the other day and I realized that I didn't ever think in a straight line, so to speak. Sometimes I'm way out to the left and then, always going forward, I might veer a little to the far right. Overall, I think it puts me more or less in the middle most of the time, which is probably a good thing. That being said, I don't think it would work to just put blinders on and run down the middle, because life has curves and we would crash into a wall for sure. And if we just let someone guide us like a racehorse on the track, we would just end up going in circles. God made us to be freethinking people and to be able to pick and choose and even change our minds. Maybe even He is re-thinking right now. And maybe, with the help of Herman Amslear, He's doing a little re-chiseling on some plates and they all start with, "Oh, by Jesus" and end that way, too.

One final thing: do you remember when they used to end all books with the words, "The End"? I changed that because Dannyl, one of my teenage granddaughters would say; "Well, duh...there aren't anymore pages, Gramps." So I'll just say, "So long, with love, Dale."